Humanistic Psychology

Humanistic Psychology

NEW FRONTIERS

Edited by
DOROTHY D. NEVILL

CALIFORNIA SCHOOL OF PROFESSIONAL PSYCHOLOGY
LOS ANGELES

GARDNER PRESS, INC., NEW YORK

Distributed by Halsted Press
Division of John Wiley & Sons, Inc.

New York · Toronto · London · Sydney

GARDNER PRESS, INC.
19 Union Square West
New York, New York 10003

Distributed exclusively by the Halsted Press Division
of John Wiley & Sons, Inc., New York

Library of Congress Cataloging in Publication Data
Main entry under title:
Humanistic psychology.
  1. Humanistic psychology. I. Nevill, Dorothy D.
BF204.H87   150'.19'2   77-23369
ISBN 0-470-99165-8

Printed in the United States of America

BOOK DESIGN BY RAYMOND SOLOMON

Preface

*A*lthough I have read many prefaces before, when it comes to writing my first one, I find myself sitting at my typewriter strangely "finger-tied." The main explanation for my hesitancy might be that the articles in this volume do not need an introduction. They were chosen to present a comprehensive view of the major issues in humanistic psychology and arranged so that a natural flow is evident from one to another. The first section deals with the integration of psychology. Art Combs lucidly explains the concepts of open and closed systems and sees the appropriateness of both. Ted Landsman gives us an historical perspective on the demise and rise of experience in the study of psychology and presents a valid claim as to the necessity of both behavior and experience in any definition of psychology. Cliff Swensen closes the section by presenting a theoretical paradigm that could encompass the broad divisions of psychology. Once the necessary inclusion of humanistic psychology in the general field of psychology is assured, it is a natural step to inquire of its philosophy. Elizabeth Simpson, after presenting a brief history of humanistic psychology, argues that concern with social issues be added to the more individualistic, self-fulfillment aspects of humanistic psychology. Ed Barker, writing in a futuristic sense, cites some of the problems of our current life patterns and the importance of humanistic values in the solving of social problems. Dorothy Nevill elects a particular issue, feminism, and draws a parallel between the principles embodied in that movement and those in the humanistic movement.

But humanistic psychology is more than a theory. It has an active component, both in its use in psychotherapy and in research. Carl Rogers recounts an episode that occurred in a large workshop and sees in it rich theoretical implications. Gene Gendlin and Jim Bugental write in depth of the therapeutic situation; the former about using experiential focusing with clients who are not getting anywhere, and the latter about the negative and positive aspects of depression. Larry Rosini gives a broad introduction to many of the relevant issues in humanistic psychological research. Franz Epting, Ed Barker, and Dave Suchman present a thorough review of research in self-disclosure, followed by Mary Horn's insightful treatise on the importance of research for both therapy and service skills.

Many of the articles in this book came from a conference held January, 1976, in memorial to Sidney M. Jourard. His work and his influence run like a golden thread throughout the entire book, binding it together. The book concludes with two tributes to him, one by a student, Marty Amerikaner, the other by a colleague, Ted Landsman.

A book such as this cannot occur without the help of many; a fact which is particularly true in this case. There were many friends and colleagues who were willing to throw me lifelines that kept my head above water and finally allowed both me and the book to reach firm ground. Chief among these friends are, of course, the authors of the various articles. They patiently endured and promptly responded to my pleas for dates and my suggestions for reworking, rearranging, and, horror of horrors, even eliminating some of their work. Particular thanks go to Larry Rosini and Mary Horn, who worked under almost unmerciful deadlines to fill that void. Two people, Ted Landsman and Franz Epting, have been with me throughout the whole project and might be even said to have initiated it by asking me to serve as chairperson of the original conference. They have been a constant source of support and encouragement: two people whom I love dearly. As I have read other acknowledgments I have often wondered as to the validity of statements such as "without whom this book couldn't have been written," but now I know exactly what is meant. Beth Stephenson has served as my assistant throughout, from the beginning of the conference and to the final stages of this book. Whether she was setting up workshops, meeting speakers, hosting a party that turned out to be the highlight of the conference, reading the manuscript countless times, researching references in the library, or doing one of the myriad of other tasks involved in an undertaking such as this, she was splendid. Thanks also should go to many other people: Merle Meyer, who in spite of a bare-bones budget was able to find release time for me. In particular I thank Toni Jourard, for her advice and enthusiasm, Therese May, for proofing the entire manuscript, and Cheryl Phillips, for endless typing and retyping.

I hope that the reading of this book will enrich your life as much as the editing of it did mine.

Dorothy D. Nevill

Gainesville, Florida

Contributors

MARTIN AMERIKANER, University of Florida

EDWIN N. BARKER, Harvard University

JAMES F. T. BUGENTAL, The Querencia

ARTHUR W. COMBS, Greely, Colorado

FRANZ EPTING, University of Florida

E. T. GENDLIN, The University of Chicago

MARY LEMKAU HORN, Counselling Associates

TED LANDSMAN, University of Florida

DOROTHY D. NEVILL, University of Florida

CARL R. ROGERS, Center for Studies of the Person

LARRY ROSINI, Harvard University

ELIZABETH LEONIE SIMPSON, University of California, Irvine

DAVID SUCHMAN, University of Florida

CLIFFORD H. SWENSEN, Purdue University

Contents

I

Toward an Integration of Psychology

1

A Choice of Futures

ARTHUR W. COMBS

*T*here are still some people in psychology who regard the humanist movement as a kind of misguided sidetrack off the main track of "real" psychology, an unsubstantial development not likely to make much contribution to psychological thought in the long run. For others, it is a point of view of interest only to applied psychology, but not really to be taken seriously as a rigorous, scientific discipline. As a consequence its proponents are often regarded as dilettantes amusing themselves with second-rate problems.

For me, the humanist movement is no flash in the pan; it is a revolution in human thought, a necessary occurrence in the sweep of human events. The Movement is expressed not just in psychology, but in all aspects of human thought: in sociology, anthropology, theology, philosophy, political science, in every aspect of human interaction. I see humanistic psychology as only the expression of this worldwide movement as it relates to the problems of human beings. The Movement calls for a whole new conception of the nature of man, his capacities and potentialities. In time its effects will even produce a new kind of man.

I see the humanist movement as the natural consequence of a crisis point in human civilization. If it had not occurred, it would have to be invented. Millions of years of human interaction with the physical and social environment have brought us to a fork in the road where it is necessary to make a choice of futures truly awesome in its full implications, frightening or exciting, depending upon one's point of view. Let me try to outline in the remainder of this chapter what it means to me for psychology.

THE CHANGING CHARACTER
OF HUMANITY'S CRUCIAL PROBLEMS

Since the dawn of human history man's greatest problems have been primarily concerned with the control of environment, finding ways of wresting from the physical world the food, clothing, and shelter required for the welfare and protection of himself and his loved ones. For millions of years this search necessarily occupied the majority of people's time and energies. For the first time in history we have in hand the power and the know-how to feed and clothe and house the entire world. In the past 200 years the fantastic advances of science have made it possible for us to understand the nature of the world we live in as never before. At the same time the Industrial Revolution and practical inventions of machinery and organization have made it possible to put that knowledge to work extracting from the environment the means to satisfy our physical needs. We have the know-how and the capability to fulfill the basic needs which have motivated human beings since the beginning of human history; only to find ourselves confronted now with even more intricate problems.

Our very success in gaining control of the environment has brought us face to face with the problems of personal being and becoming, and of people's relationships with each other. We have created a world in which we are, all of us, more interrelated and interdependent than any society in the history of the world. We are utterly dependent on the cooperative effort and goodwill of other human beings so that few of us could live for more than a few hours out of touch with our fellows. We are totally dependent on the cooperative effort of millions of other people to provide us with the simplest necessities of daily life. What is more, the very powers we have created to solve our physical problems can also be used disastrously in the hands of a drunken driver, a Lee Harvey Oswald, or power-mad tyrants unconcerned for the welfare of others. The greatest problems of our time are now human problems: how to live with ourselves and each other in a world growing smaller and smaller. Problems of distribution, pollution, population, crime in the streets, terror, violation of human rights, and many more are essentially human problems. It is not atomic bombs we fear, but the people who might use them.

CLOSED AND OPEN SYSTEMS OF THOUGHT

Two broad general choices for dealing with human problems are available to us. Each is a way of thinking about dealing with human events and each has its inevitable consequences for action. Each also calls for its own psychological theory and practice. They are often described as closed and open systems of thinking.

The closed system is one in which the final product is known in advance and machinery is established to reach that objective. This is the approach one would use in planning an itinerary. It is also the approach used in industry to achieve the production of products or by teachers who desire to teach a child that two and two is four. One defines his goals, establishes the machinery to reach them, puts the machinery in operation, then assesses the outcomes to determine, if, indeed, the objective was achieved. An open system, on the other hand, may begin without a manifest objective. It may simply confront a problem, then search for solutions the nature of which cannot clearly be discerned in the beginning. This is the approach counselors use in assisting a client to explore a problem. It is also the system employed in a legislature debating an issue, or in modern "discovery" approaches to teaching.

Whichever system one chooses for dealing with human events inevitably commits him to a whole series of consequences having to do with the problems selected for attention, psychological theories used as guides to action, ways of regarding participants, techniques for dealing with them, responsibilities for action, as well as philosophical and moral implications. Let us examine some of these briefly.

The Goals of Open and Closed Systems

In a closed system of thinking ends are known in advance. Goals can be clearly defined, often with high degrees of precision. Problems can be examined, dealt with objectively, and subjected to precise methods of measurement or assessment. Problems have clear beginnings and ends, and goals can often be stated as "oughts" or "shoulds." Applied to human problems, closed systems call for establishment of behavioral objectives expressed in terms of specific acts or behaviors. The precision made possible by precise statement of objectives in behavioral terms makes closed systems highly attractive to legislators, managers, taxpayers, and the general public. Closed systems seem straightforward and businesslike, and provide a comforting illusion of accuracy and precision.

The goals of open systems cannot be so precisely defined, for outcomes will often be unknown in advance, existing only as holistic objectives capable of statement only in generalized terms. In counseling, for example, client and counselor goals may be to help a client become more clearly aware of himself or to improve his marital relationships. Just how that will come about neither counselor nor client can perceive at the start of the counseling process.

Open systems are discovery-oriented. They seek not to prove, but to find out. Sometimes the explorations involved in the process may even be more important than the outcomes. Open systems may also be much more subjective than closed ones, and so are more applicable to problems having to do with the internal life of human beings, matters like feelings, attitudes, beliefs, values, and human fears, loves, and aspirations. Open-system goals often cannot be precisely determined and may even change in the course of operations, for example, when students pursuing one line of study discover fascinating new problems for exploration not even suspected in the beginning of study. Seen from an outsider's point of view the lack of precisely defined outcomes is often misconstrued as mystical, vague, or even irresponsible.

Techniques Employed in Closed and Open Systems

Kurt Lewin (1931) once discussed what he called "Aristotelian" and "Gallilean" approaches to the building of psychological theory. He described Aristotelian theory building as a systematic attempt to build basic principles one on another much in the fashion of a mason building a house. The process is one of establishing precisely known items bit by bit, then fitting these together in larger and larger patterns. He described the Gallilean approach as more like the opening up of an unexplored territory. Explorers arrive on an unknown shore and penetrate tentatively into the interior. As exploration proceeds these first trails become paths, paths then become roads that eventually become highways until the new territory has been mapped and understood in all its ramifications. These two positions are much like the closed and open systems I have been talking about.

Closed systems proceed in highly objective ways to deal with problems in step by step fashion in precisely defined orderly, logical sequence. Open systems operate in more subjective ways. Ends are unknown in advance; thus machinery cannot be neatly designed to reach them. Instead, open systems must rely on the intelligence and motivation of people to confront problems and to discover appropriate solutions. Exploration is search for the unknown. If one is not certain about what he is looking for, the guidelines for seeking must necessarily concentrate on processes, those principles governing the confrontation of problems and the facilitation of exploration. The techniques required to operate in open systems must, therefore, concentrate on creating conditions conducive to effective problem solving.

This process orientation of open systems causes them to be grossly misunderstood in a society like ours that worships objectivity, production, and the scientific method. Compared to the nice, neat, straightforward businesslike efficiency of closed systems, the operations of open ones seem dreadfully vague and imprecise. Examined from the frame of reference of a closed system, open systems are often criticized as mystical, unsystematic, or unscientific, and its practitioners may be described as moonstruck, irresponsible dreamers out of touch with reality. Ask a closed-system worker what he is up to, and one gets nice, neat statements for answers. Ask a humanist what he is after, and he confuses you with talk about processes, conditions, and what people think and feel about matters. Closed systems have such comforting illusions of certainty, whereas open approaches seem dangerously permissive or devious.

Few people understand that a system is not good or bad in its own right. A system is only a device for assuring the achievement of one's objectives. Applied to the wrong objectives, a system may only guarantee that one's errors will be colossal. Unfortunately, that fact is not widely known, and the general public continues to regard events that provide the illusion of neatness, order, and system as practically synonymous with goodness or rightness. This is the cross open-system thinkers must bear and seems unlikely to be dissipated at any time in the near future.

Regard for Persons
in Open and Closed Systems

Closed systems are product-oriented. As a consequence, persons involved tend to be regarded as part of the machinery by which the product is produced. The behavior of persons is paramount, and persons are likely to be treated as objects to be moulded or shaped in preconceived ways. Such a view of human beings is a natural outgrowth of an objective approach to human problems. Objectivity is a way of looking at people characteristic of our society. We take it in with our mother's milk. We are controlled and managed throughout our school years. We live in an industrial society and admire the efficiency and precision with which our manufacturing giants provide us with an almost inexhaustible river of goods and services. We worship science and the "scientific method" as a sacred cow. Even our religions have taught us to treat ourselves as objects as they exhort us to "make yourself be good." In a closed system of thinking the important thing about people is not their personness, but their behavior, what they do, and how they can be so managed to achieve desired outcomes with the greatest possible efficiency.

Open systems have a different regard for persons. Persons are not the machinery by which the product is produced; persons are, themselves, the product. Failure to understand this fact has caused enormous mischief throughout our society as we have tried to apply the objective industrial model to human institutions. Education, for example, is currently suffering immensely from well-intentioned efforts to increase efficiency by the application of methods that have worked so well in the production of goods in industry. The effort is doomed to failure because the model is not appropriate. Persons in our schools, as in other human institutions, are not parts of the machinery producing a product, persons *are* the product, and whatever models we adopt for dealing with them must be appropriate to that fundamental fact. If industry were truly organized for the welfare of the worker, our great corporations surely would not be organized the way they are. Open systems call for patterns of organization based on the psychology of human being and becoming. Persons are regarded as dynamic rather than static processes. The problems confronted and the solutions accepted are judged in terms of the persons involved. Success or failure is measured in terms of human satisfactions, values, and feelings.

The ways in which persons are regarded in closed and open systems have inevitable effects on the ways participants react. For example, regarding people as objects is likely to result in lack of commitment and the separation of persons into categories of managers and workers, teachers and students, doctors and patients, and the like. Being regarded as objects, in turn, is likely to produce feelings of dehumanization and alienation accompanied by the labeling of each group by the other as the "enemy." This state of affairs was the genesis of the labor movement. As workers felt increasingly dehumanized and alienated, they learned to band together in unions to beat the system. The same processes now seem to be going on in social institutions like education, political action, and social work. Of course, there are times when the question of what persons in the systems think of each other is a matter of no great concern. It is dangerous, however, to behave as though such concomitants did not exist. Such ignorance can, and often does, have disastrous consequences, resulting in the sabotage of the best laid plans.

The effects of open systems are far more salutary. Because persons are regarded as dynamic forces, their participation is active rather than passive. Because they participate in decision, commitment is far less of a problem, and responsibility for personal action is more likely to be a consequence. Motivation is inherent in the problems, themselves, and need not be applied from without. Because persons are valued as individuals, personal effort is greater and creativity a more frequent outcome. A sense of teamwork and identification is more likely in an open system with a greater degree of caring for fellow participants.

The Problem of Control
in Closed and Open Systems

Responsibility for operations is quite different in closed and open systems. In a closed system responsibility is lodged in directors, managers, or administrators responsible for seeing to it that ends are properly achieved. The model is similar to the medical model with which most of us are familiar. One goes to the doctor and states his problem. The doctor then diagnoses the situation, determines the goals to be achieved, and writes a prescription for the patient, who is expected to carry out the doctor's orders. Responsibility for control and direction of the process is almost exclusively that of the doctor, with the patient in a passive or subservient role. The model is also familiar in the structure of modern industry, the military, and many other of our institutions.

The emphasis of a closed system is on the achievement of preconceived goals. The task of the manager is to expedite progress toward those ends. To do this well managers must be expert diagnosticians, who know at any moment precisely what is going on and where events must be channeled next. This places a terrible responsibility on the managerial group. Having defined the ends to be sought, they also have total responsibility for outcomes. In the medical profession this leads to the principle of "total responsibility" for the patient. It can also be observed in industry, where bosses are held responsible for production quotas and the behavior of workers.

Such "expert" roles place a heavy burden on closed-system leaders. The necessity for being an expert diagnostician is a two-edged sword. On the one hand, it endows the leader with a special aura. It provides him respect and admiration for superior talent and know-how from others and personal feelings of power over people and events. This is a heady business. History has been replete with horrible examples of leaders blinded by such adoration who came to believe it was justly deserved. Leadership in a closed system is a terrible responsibility. Managers cannot be wrong. They *have* to be right. As a consequence, closed-system managers often live in constant fear of failure, which may result in the covering up of mistakes, or continuous efforts to defend against the possibilities of failure by conservatism and defense of the status quo in the belief that taking no action runs no risks.

Closed systems tend to result in a society characterized by a concentration of power vested in a highly professional and intellectual elite, a managerial class. This special class, in turn, tends to form a network linking major agencies and organizations together. Much time and effort is spent on the search for better and better models, devices for making systems work. This effect can be observed in current attempts to apply computer technology and "systems" approaches to all kinds of human problems.

Leadership in a closed system is often a lonely role. Not many people can stand on top of a pedestal, so that opportunities for intimate human contacts become increasingly difficult. Relationships with other people also become distorted by the consequences of the superiority-inferiority role definition imposed by a closed system. It is a normal human reaction to fear those with authority over us and just as normal to find ways of defending one's self against those threats. In consequence, closed system-leaders must spend much time and effort attempting to deal one way or another with other persons whose attitudes are likely to be apathetic, passive, or covertly or overtly hostile.

Open systems have a quite different locus of responsibility. Because operations are problem-centered rather than ends-oriented, products are not known in advance. Responsibility for outcomes, therefore, is not centered in a leader or manager; it is shared by all who confront the problem. This jointly shared responsibility removes a great burden from leadership. Leaders do not *have* to be right. Mistakes need not be seen as disastrous calamities or evidence of personal failure. They can be taken in stride as normal, even acceptable, aspects of the process.

The emphasis of open systems is on participation with sharing of power and decision making. The role of the leader in such a system is not director, but facilitator whose expertise is expressed in the advancement of processes, in creating conditions conductive to movement. This role is not manager, but minister, not director, but helper, aid, assistant, or consultant to an ongoing process. Such an emphasis calls for cooperation rather than competition and expertise in helping and facilitating the processes of interaction.

The facilitating role of leadership in an open system has its inevitable effects on the relationship between leader and group. Because responsibility for outcomes is shared, the leader is freed from the necessity to be right. This is no mean consideration and makes possible the operation of leadership in far more relaxed, open, humane fashion. Success in an open system is dependent on the cooperation of persons and the facilitation of processes. This makes the leader a helper or participant, and such roles are likely to result in far more satisfactory interpersonal relationships between leaders and groups. Leaders are not so likely to be regarded as the enemy to be sabotaged or fawned on. They can be identified with as aids, assistants, or as friendly representatives of society, possessed of valuable and helpful skills for advancing the achievement of group purposes. Leaders can be treated as fellow human beings in such circumstances and related to without fear of the loss of one's own identity. Leaders in an open system have much more chance of relating to others in warm and human terms, and of being regarded by those they work with, with respect and affection. They can probably like themselves better as well.

Philosophical Implications of Closed and Open Systems

The choice of systems we make for dealing with human events also commits us to quite different philosophical positions. These are often not clear in isolated or simple application. Pursued to their logical conclusions, however, they result in quite different philosophical positions. For example, closed-system operations depend on management and control of affairs by a management class. To operate effectively in a closed system, goals must be known in advance. Someone must decide the outcomes to be sought. This leads directly to a "great man" philosophy, someone "who knows where the people should go" so that the rest of us can set up the machinery to make certain they get there. Carried to its logical extreme, such a concept leads directly to a dictatorship.

Open systems of thinking result in a quite different philosophy and social organization. Open systems are egalitarian. Persons involved in such systems are regarded as possessing innate worth and the capacity to find their own solutions. Open systems are essentially democratic. The basic concept of democracy holds that "when men are free, they can find their own best ways." This is also the open-system position for dealing with human problems. The big "if" in the democratic philosophy, of course, is the phrase "when men are free." To provide that freedom is the very reason for existence of open-system approaches to human problems. From my point of view, one of the comforting things about dealing with problems from an open-system approach is its congruence with the democratic philosophy. My psychology is not basically out of touch with my philosophy.

The Psychology of Closed and Open Systems

The purpose of theory in science is to order information in ways that make it useful for dealing with problems. It is not surprising, therefore, that closed and open systems of thinking have each been accompanied by appropriate positions in psychological theory. Behavioral psychology is the natural outcome of closed systems of thinking. It provides a valuable framework for understanding human behavior in objective terms. Behavioral approaches do much more; they provide a frame of reference for dealing with human problems in precise, goal-oriented terms. Behavioral psychology is "what the doctor ordered" for closed systems of thinking.

Open systems, too, require appropriate psychological theory. This need is currently expressed in half a dozen varieties of humanistic psychology. These new psychologies are expressly designed to deal with the subjective questions posed in open-system thinking and provide the framework needed especially for understanding the internal life of human beings. Humanistic psychology is, thus, a normal and necessary outcome of the need to confront human problems from an open system of thinking.

Earl Kelley once said about setting things up in dichotomies, "Whenever you find ideas expressed at opposite ends of a continuum in either-or fashion, it is almost certain they are both wrong." I am sure there are many who will complain that my contrast of closed and open systems is much too dramatic or extreme. I would be the first to agree. My statement is, indeed, stark, sketchy, and open to argument or contrary interpretation. I have not intended this discussion to be definitive. I have used this contrast primarily as an illustration of the very important principle that whatever approaches we take to thinking about human problems inevitably commit us to events that stretch far beyond the immediate point of action. For this discussion whether the detailed points of my analysis are accurate is not the crucial issue. The important point is simply this: that our choice of closed or open systems leads inevitably to ramifications far beyond a simple commitment. That is true for everyone. For psychologists, it has a further message: namely, the choice we make for approaching human problems will also determine the theories of psychology we construct, the problems we seek to explore, the techniques we use for research and application, even the nature and value of our contributions to human welfare.

THE EMERGENCE OF OPEN SYSTEMS

For generations we have lived in the era of physical science. Closed-system thinking has provided the means for fantastic strides toward human control of the environment around us. Through its contributions we have learned to control the physical world about us as never before, only to find ourselves confronted now with the human problems of how to understand ourselves and live effectively with one another. We have passed from the era of physical science to the era of social science. With that passing we are also in the process of shifting our primary ways of thinking from closed systems to open ones. New problems call for new ways of thinking and theory building.

As Maslow (1962) has pointed out, human needs exist in a kind of hierarchy from those primary needs for food, air, and water to high-level needs like fulfillment and actualization. Because human needs are insatiable, the satisfaction of lower needs simply sets us free to seek higher ones. A man with an empty belly is not likely to be intrigued with nice thoughts about democracy. But with physical needs fulfilled, one can turn his attention to questions of personal fulfillment, growth, and actualization. Thus the very successes of science and industry have within them the seeds of their own succession as primary sources of human-need satisfaction. The more they provide us with goods and services and control over our environment, the more they set us free to seek satisfaction of personal humanistic needs. Seen in the light of these events, the humanistic movement is no accident. It is an inevitable consequence of basic changes in human civilization itself.

Closed-system thinking by itself is no longer adequate for the solution of human problems. Closed systems were highly appropriate for dealing with the physical world or dealing with human beings as objects. To deal with the human problems of our time we shall have to rely increasingly on open systems of thinking. Objectivity and closed systems of thinking are the tools of physical science and have brought us far in the control of the physical world. Subjectivity and open systems of thinking are the new tools of social science and the humanist movement increasingly required to deal with our pressing new problems.

The great human problems we face can be dealt with only in part by closed systems of thinking. The problems of people cannot be met by neat definable solutions. A good example of this is to be found in the field of education. For more than a hundred years education in America was able to live with a curriculum designed for everyone. The purpose of schools was to prepare students for the future, and we knew what children would need to know. The rapidity of change in the modern world has destroyed all that. We no longer know what students will need to know tomorrow. In addition, the information explosion characteristic of the last 20 or 30 years has settled for all time the idea that educators will ever again be able to establish a curriculum for everyone. The modern goal for education can no longer be defined in such neat, precise terms. The best we can do is to seek the production of intelligent persons, people capable of confronting new problems and finding solutions adequate for the time and place they live in. Such a goal requires an open system of thinking and a more comprehensive psychology as well.

It is no longer enough to deal with people as objects, to concern ourselves solely with externally observable behavior. This is much too narrow a view to cope with current human problems. The time is long past due for an open system of psychology capable of handling the subjective experiential problems of being and becoming posed by the modern world. The humanistic movement is no accident. It has come into being precisely because it was needed to fill the needs of our time.

The emergence of humanism has not always been understood or appreciated. There are many who see traditional approaches to psychology and humanism as matters of either-or. Psychologists are defined as "behaviorists" or "humanists" and then assumed to be deadly enemies of one another. Sometimes this assumption is real, more's the pity, but such internecine warfare is childish and arrogant. It is also a dreadful waste of time and talent better spent on more significant activity. The fact of the matter is, psychology needs *both* behaviorist and humanist views if it is to have any hope of contributing to current needs, or of realizing its own destiny. Mathematicians do not describe themselves as "arithmetists," "algebraists," or "calculists" and fight for supremacy of those theoretical positions. They recognize arithmetic, algebra, and calculus as theoretical frameworks useful and necessary for dealing with different kinds of problems.

The purpose of theory is to make it possible to deal effectively with problems. It is time we recognized that behaviorism and humanism are only tools for dealing with psychological problems. A professional worker who has two tools at his command is far more likely to find good solutions to his problems than the worker with only one. When a student comes to my office to inquire what he must do to demonstrate his competence I tell him clearly, straightforwardly in stimulus-response terms. I clearly define the goals and procedures to be met in behavioral terms. The same student on another occasion who comes to my office in deep distress because he is not getting along with his wife finds me behaving in humanist terms employing the open systems of effective counseling.

It is time we understood that humanism is here to stay, because it is an absolutely necessary invention to cope with changing human needs. Just as mathematicians developed algebra to deal with events not adequately handled by arithmetic, so humanism is the algebra of psychology, come into being to deal more efficiently with those problems not adequately handled by traditional approaches. To recognize this fact psychology must redefine itself.

The definition of psychology as the study of human and animal behavior with which we have lived for almost a century is no longer adequate. An examination of a dictionary will show that psychology is generally defined in two ways: first, as the "study of mental states and processes" and second, as the "study of human and animal behavior." Psychology began with the first of those definitions, the "study of mental states and processes." With the coming of physical science, however, American psychology became, almost exclusively, limited to the study of human and animal behavior, because those problems were amenable to the methods of physical science. Meanwhile the study of mental states and processes was largely ignored or derided as legitimate aspects of psychological study. In a very real sense the humanist movement represents a return to the original, primary definition of psychology. Defining psychology exclusively as the "study of behavior" is no longer enough. Psychology needs a new definition as *"the study of persons, encompassing (a) mental states and processes and (b) human and animal behavior."* This definition may help us truly appreciate our varied talents and concepts and bring us together as psychologists all. With such a definition we can mobilize all our resources to confront the pressing problems of our times with ever-increasing effectiveness.

We stand at a moment of choice. Two alternative ways of thinking about human problems are before us. We can opt for closed systems and the second-phase industrial society it leads to, or we can choose an open system and a person-centered society. The choice, of course, is not entirely either-or. Both ways of dealing with human events will sometimes be appropriate, depending on the nature of the problems we confront. No matter which choice we make, we shall of necessity experience times and conditions requiring the other alternative. The choice we confront is a larger matter of overall values. The problem is one of perspective. The danger lies in committing ourselves to frames of reference without full awareness of the consequences of our choices.

The destinies of men have always been moulded by the problems they confronted and the beliefs that guided them in seeking solutions. The ways we think about dealing with human problems inevitably affect the questions we confront, the choices we make, the goals we seek, the processes we create, even the institutions we build far into the future. When beliefs have been clear and accurate, great strides have been made. But history is also replete with terrible examples of what can happen to people whose actions are predicated on false or inaccurate assumptions.

Psychology's charge as a social science is to provide us with the clearest, most accurate understandings of the nature of the persons and their interactions possible in our generation. How well we meet that responsibility will depend on the choices we make for thinking about our problems. Each of us is free to make his choice. As professional psychologists, however, none of us is free to make those choices lightly or without full knowledge of their concomitant implications.

I have made my choice. I have chosen open systems of thought and the humanist movement in psychology because I believe they provide the most effective guidelines for my way of life, for my interrelationships with other people and the most promising frame of reference for thinking about the pressing problems of our time. I have grown up with the humanist movement. I have lived to see it first reviled and rejected, then, bit by bit, adopted by one outstanding psychologist after another over the past 30 years. Speaking here in Gainesville in 1961, Abe Maslow expressed his belief that humanistic psychology would live to become "The Psychology" by another 20 years. I doubted Abe's forecast then, but the older I get, the more I think he was right.

References

Kelley, E. Personal communication.

Lewin, K. The conflict between Aristotelian and Galilean modes of thought in contemporary psychology. *Journal of Genetic Psychology*, 1931, 5, 141–177.

Maslow, A. H. Comments at the *First Annual Conference on Personality Theory and Counseling Practice*, University of Florida, Gainesville, Florida, 1961.

Maslow, A. H. *Toward a psychology of being*. Princeton, N.J.: Van Nostrand, 1962.

2

Psychology as the Science of Behavior *and* Experience

TED LANDSMAN

*T*he new growth spurt of humanistic psychology and a parallel emergence of behavior modification therapies create a new need for some historical clarification of both the past conceptions of psychology and the contemporary confusions concerning reconceptualization. The argument centers solely about three words: psychology, behavior, and experience.

The definition of psychology has been remarkably varied over the less than 100 years of its formal scientific history. This has never been a static profession, and it has prided itself on its history of change. However, any one young psychologist at any one period might find it necessary to commit himself with passion to the particular contemporary definition. We smile nowadays over the quaintness in the prescience period of the first definition, "the study of the soul."

   The forum wherein psychology receives its official definition and conceptualization is not the annual meetings, but the general or introductory psychology textbook, which very few college sophomores have escaped over those past 100 years. James Baldwin (1890) writing about the time of the founding of the Wundtian laboratory defined it as the "science of phenomena of consciousness" (p. 8). William James (1892) and J. R. Angell (1908) used essentially the same terminology; the former opening his famous book *Psychology* with the definition stated as: "the description and explanation of states of consciousness as such" (p. 1); the latter presented the briefer definition, "the science of consciousness" (p. 1).

   From 1910, through World War I and into World War II, vigorous disagreement pervades the textbooks. Watsonian behaviorism attracted great attention, but by no means did it really intimidate the undergraduates and their teachers who defended the romance in the subject matter. Titchener (1902), an unquestioned giant in our history, called it the "science of mental processes" (p. 7) and Watson (1914) made an indelible and not at all colorful mark upon the science with the assertion that the subject matter of human psychology is the behavior of the human beings. McDougall (1921), thought by many to be an antagonist to Watson, claimed an even earlier origin to the term. He reports that in 1905, seven years before Watson, he had defined psychology as "the positive science of conduct or behavior" (p. 15). Succeeding writers referred to varying forms of "mind" or "mental activities," but Howard C. Warren (1922) advanced a definition of which I want to make special note: "systematic study of man's daily experience" (p. 1).

   Many contemporary psychologists studied Robert S. Woodworth as a text first in 1921 then through various editions. Some psychologists still flourishing, but of even riper vintage, taught using that textbook. Woodworth's description was: "the science of the conscious and near-conscious activities of the living individual" (p. 17). Did he really mean, however, the *behavior* of the individual?

   Perrin and Klein (1926) suggested "control and prediction of behavior" (p. 16). Weld (1928) was one of the few who acknowledged the confusion. He suggested four different definitions, varying from the mental phenomena or phenomena of consciousness to the mind-body dualism. Other definitions include Weatherhead (1935), "science of behavior" (p. 2); Guilford (1939), another grand old name, "science of mental activity of organisms" (p. 3); Knight Dunlap (1936) suggests another direction, "the science of the responses of the individual to his environment" (p. 17); Averill (1943), "science of human mind and behavior" (p. 5).

We come now to one of the great classics in textbooks, Boring, Langfeld, and Weld (1948). This text was respected by professors for the dignity and scholarship of its senior author and by students who were endlessly amused by their own observations that the name of the senior author so aptly described the book's contents. In *Foundations of Psychology* the authors' suggestion was "the study of human nature" (p. 1) followed by the explanation: "psychology deals with both the behavior of man as it appears in his responses and with consciousness as he finds it in his immediate experience" (p. 4).

Booksellers report that one of the most popular textbooks of all times and of all fields was that by Norman Munn (1951), *Psychology: The Fundamentals of Human Adjustments.* In the 1951 edition he defined the field with this explanation: "the scientific investigation of behavior, including, from the standpoint of behavior, much of what earlier psychologists dealt with as experience" (p. 23).

From then on texts by Hill (1970), Hebb (1966), even Munn's (1969) edition, Morgan and King (1971), and Ruch and Zimbardo (1971) more or less describe psychology as we know it today as "the science of behavior," perhaps the simplest definition of all the sciences, not even a "one-liner," or a "half-liner" description. It possesses exquisite parsimony and sharpness, clarity and nonambiguity in a field that has striven a century long for the cleanliness of physics' definition of its subject matter, which is exactly that: the study of matter. Despite all this, here we are now again, attempting to befuddle the definition. Are we trying to drag psychology, screaming and kicking, back into the nineteenth century?

Surely, many still recall being entertained in first lectures with the "fun" statement that "psychology once lost its soul, then lost its consciousness, and now has lost its mind?" But it has never lost its "behavior," perhaps because there is no way one can say that and make it funny.

It appears, among other things, that from 1920 to 1950, the profession was greatly stimulated by diversity, largely initiated by the insistent and rebellious behaviorists. After 1950 psychology lost its diversity and gained a false unanimity. For perhaps some 30 years, during which psychology as a profession was rapidly maturing as a science, there was increasing discomfort with the apologetic deferences to the concept of human experience.

Definitions of psychology as simply "the science of behavior," although elegant, neat, pure, virtuous, and unambiguous, are not truly parsimonious; they are impoverished. They function first to exclude an enormous subject matter that is necessary to understand, predict, control, and *enjoy* behavior. In such an exclusion these definors serve to reduce the possibility of sound, meaningful research being generated with the data of experience, the "other half" of psychology's subject matter. This is not a new argument, but in this golden age of behaviorism it needs to be restated and to be reasserted.

There was a time when the shoe was on the other foot. There are those humanists who, like many contemporary behaviorists, are certain that the truth lies only in experience and its components. They hope to demonstrate to the rest of the academic world that some kind of purity in experiential or phenomenological methodology will yield greater fruits to those who labor in that vineyard; but in such are more likely the barren harvests of 1903 when consciousness alone was permitted as the subject matter.

What reaction might the following paragraph excite today?

We have been accused of being propagandists, of heralding our conclusions in the public press rather than in the more dignified scientific journals, of writing as though no one else had ever contributed to the field of psychology of being bolshevists.

Having been brought up on *behavioristic* psychology, as most of us have, you naturally ask these questions and you will find it hard to put away the old terminology and begin to formulate your psychological life in terms of *humanism. Humanism* is new wine and it will not go into old bottles. It is advisable for the time being to allay your natural antagonism and accept the *humanistic* platform at least until you get more deeply into it. Later you will find that you have progressed so far with *humanism* that the questions you now raise will answer themselves in a perfectly satisfactory natural science way. Let me hasten to add that if the *humanist* were to ask you what you mean by the (objective) terms you have been in the habit of using, I could soon make you tongue-tied with contradictions. He could even convince you that you do not know what you mean by them.

I think you would agree that this sounds like a typical argument of one of our extreme humanists. The quotations, with only two words altered, "humanism" and "behavioristic," to replace each other, is taken from Watson's 1930 edition of *Behaviorism* (p. *vi* and p. 10). A different traveler slept then in the procrustean bed.

I see no immediate danger of psychology returning to the 1930s under pressure from the humanists. I do see the possibility of a great waste of effort and many angry exercises in futility on the part of extremists, some jealously protecting the half-line definition hard won over the past 30 years and others struggling to substitute "experience" for "behavior." Either extreme alone constitutes a plague upon the only house of psychology.

THE LEXICOLOGY OF "BEHAVIOR"

All the major lexicological psychologists, English and English (1958), Warren (1934), Harriman (1947), Eysenck, Arnold, and Meili (1972), separately and together reflect the frantic and largely chaotic "conspiracy" to present a totally objective view of the subject matter of psychology and yet not completely alienate the large group of us who stubbornly maintain the accessibility of our science to subjective phenomena.

The multiple personality thus given the profession is reflected in the terms used in their definitions of behavior: "anything an animal does" (English & English, 1958, p. 61); "all modes of muscular or glandular response" (Warren, 1934, p. 30); "anything whatsoever that is done by a living organism, includes mental activities" (Harriman, 1947, p. 48).

Eysenck et al. (1972) use terms that are particularly frantic: "the activity of an organism . . . the observable activity . . . the measurable activity of a specific organism, the responses . . . a specific response movement or movement" (p. 117, V. 1).

His eighth attempt, one gets the feeling, should be preceded by, "oh, well, then": "the total activity, subjective, and objective, non-observable and observable, of an individual or a group" (p. 117, V. 1).

All the lexicographers have included mental or consciousness type of activity in their definitions, albeit in most instances indirectly with a feeling of uncleanliness. Warren (1934) adds: "these uses are confusing and are not favored" (p. 30). English and English (1958) add a hopeful note: "actually nearly all who use the term behavior seem to be referring to the same or nearly the same phenomena, despite their differences in conceiving these phenomena" (p. 61).

In brief, each of us presently teaching the subject could in reasonably good conscience choose his own favored meaning, which, strange to discover within so strict and rigorous a science, could permit two such instructors to use meanings that are opposites within or between psychological theories.

I find inescapable the conclusion that the use of both terms, behavior and experience, is necessary properly to lay the conceptual framework of the subject matter of the science of psychology. It is not alone for purposes of scientific dialogue that I press this point. The ambiguity being squeezed into the word behavior permits many narrow-minded psychologists to create an atmosphere in their graduate departments which places research in experience as beyond the pale. Thus younger psychologists, those, for example, setting much of their life style of research in their dissertations, are discouraged from looking into this forbidden, forever locked, dark, red chamber. This I find offensive not only to a science but to the twin masters it serves: truth and knowledge.

FURTHER EFFORTS TO BRING INTERNAL STATES INTO BEHAVIOR

During the 30 years of transition some, such as Munn (1969), sought to stretch the meaning of behavior to include certain internal states, such as sensation, perception, and cognition. Any effort on my part to discredit these efforts would be somewhat self-serving. The behaviorists of today are willing to accept as subject matter any such internal states that immediately seem to lend themselves to external observation, instrumentation, direct measurement, and so forth. Just prior to Watson's time, the only acceptable method for study of these states was introspection, and thus he rejected even those internal states that are a fully respected part of the conceptual matrix of the science today. However, going beyond this, I should like to point out that "experience" more characteristically describes these events or phenomena and, second, that "experience" in even its broadest senses and meanings is available to observation in an approximation of directness which gives sufficient promise to restore it to the subject matter of science.

THE DEFINITION OF EXPERIENCE

Meat for our enemies and our friends is found in Titchener's venerable *Outline of Psychology* (1902). He concludes the classic with a great appreciation for this concept:

The metaphysics to which science points us is rather a metaphysics in which both matter and spirit disappear, to make way for the unitary conception of experience (p. 366). The psychologist cannot long hesitate between the choices offered to him. The philosophy of experience points him to his place along side of the physicist and the chemist; justifies his working principle as an adumbration of the real relation of "mental" to "bodily;" and brings down philosophy itself from the clouds of speculation, to serve as a guide and director of scientific progress. As man of science, he is dealing with an organism,—with an organized structure, with a system of functions, with a developing whole; he has no concern with ultimates. As philosopher, reflecting upon the data and methods and results of science and scientific enquiry, he finds a resting place for thought in experience,—than which, as Shadworth Hodgson says, there is no longer word (pp. 367–368).

What an elegant statement. I considered changing the title of this paper to "Than Which There is No Larger Word." But then

Titchener goes on, I regret to report, for two more lines to say, "and but for which we have in the last resort no means or materials for framing any hypothesis whatsoever" (p. 368). And thus ends his book, two lines too long.

Similarly, Boring (1950), perhaps the last giant in psychology who fully appreciated both behavior and experience, in his still classic *History of Experimental Psychology* concludes his first chapter on "The Rise of Modern Science" with a tribute to phenomenology, a term for which you might substitute "experience." "At any rate," he says concluding his first chapter somewhat laconically, "phenomenology comes first" (p. 21). But like his teacher, Titchener, he adds, "even though it does not get far by itself" (p. 21).

In contrast to our historical distortion of the term "behavior," the term "experience" is largely used in psychology and philosophy quite in accordance with lay usage.

G. D. Wilson in the *Encyclopedia of Psychology*, edited by Eysenck, Arnold, and Meili (1972) presents a credible definition: "the subjective (conscious) appreciation of stimulus events, or the knowledge resulting from this; or as a verb: to live through, meet with, find, feel undergo, or be aware of any stimulus object, sensation or internal event." He adds: "Hence the term is used in psychology today in the same way as in everyday language" (p. 343). I intentionally omitted his opening sentence to give it emphasis here: "believed by many to be the best term to describe the subject matter of psychology." I am happy with this definition, with the ones given in both standard dictionaries, which, incidentally, take up about seven inches of space as contrasted to our one inch devoted to "psychology."

For clarification within the profession one should include within the general term "experience" all concepts describing the so-called internal states, phenomenological terms, even the existential conditons: sensations, perception, cognition, (about which there is no argument as to their inclusion in the subject matter of psychology) but also awareness, consciousness, feelings, personal meanings, the self, self-concept, dreams, anxiety, emotions. Thus both the unit responses to stimuli and the organized states or conditions comprised of these various responses, which may precede, be concomitant to, or follow what we ordinarily know as behavior, are to be included.

Thus when the subject sees someone across a crowded room and "flies to her side," we would study and describe the images falling on the retina, the amount of light in the room, the auditory cues, the intensity, loudness in decibels of the music, increase in blood pressure, palmar sweating, and the locomotion (rather than flying) of the organism to her side, but also the feelings of excitement, the aesthetic delight, the onrush of feelings of love, of self-doubt, or longing, wishing, seeking, hoping, all of which are part of his psychology of the moment, his behavior, and his experience. These are events, data, phenomena, not just bathwater!

The admissibility of these states (which, incidentally, should not be confused with the Titchenerian and phenomenological definitions of consciousness as being free of inference or interpretation) has always been dependent on their amenability to more or less objective study. Those ancestral heroes of ours, who either reluctantly or gleefully accepted the surrender of the early introspectionists, implied a promise of reconsideration should such conditions be met. The time is here or near.

A rich variety of experiences has been studied: psychologically critical turning point experiences (Fuerst, 1965), positive experiences (Landsman, 1968), helpful and nonhelpful experience (Pennell, 1969), intense experiences (Lynch, 1968), the experiences of blackness (Hayes, 1969), the prison experience (Smith, 1973), the experience of being fulfilled (Paul, 1968), the experience of being understood and of being misunderstood (Baggett, 1967), and the experience of transcending one's usual capacity (Privette, 1964). These experiences have been explored through the medium of a straightforward questionnaire, in which the subject is simply asked to report his or her experience, anonymously. These questionnaire reports in general, at present, represent the basic data of the entire series of studies.

One may always raise the question concerning the greater desirability of the direct observation of the experience and even of the validity of the original experience. Discussion of these issues will follow. But first, in the long tradition of the phenomenologists, one must directly read a few of these data, to gain a first-hand experience with them—perhaps in order to generate a personal judgement concerning both their significance as psychological data and their validity.

In a recent study by Smith (1973) on black and white female prisoner experience, a white inmate writes:

The third most intense experience of my life was the three weeks of my trial. I was arrested for a crime I knew nothing about. When my case came to trial, the evidence they had could have pinpointed me or any one of a dozen people. I was the unfortunate one. I sat thru my trial with the knowledge that I was not guilty. On the advice of my attorney I did not say anything to police or reporters. As the trial came closer to an end, I was convinced that the jury would find me innocent. The most horrifying experience of my life was when the jury came back into the courtroom and the judge read the paper. They had found me guilty. Please believe me when I tell you, it took every ounce of will power humanly possible not to break down. This put me in a complete state of shock. There was talk of probation because of the lack of evidence and the tremendous amount of publicity. So my spirits were lifted. Then I went to be sentenced and the judge gave me life imprisonment. This to me, after finally being completely happy and contented with my life in the past few years, was about the lowest blow I could sustain. On the short drive to prison I started thinking I am not going to let this get me down because I had one other experience that was worse. (p. 130)

Another kind of experience, taken from our collection of fulfillment experiences (Paul, 1968), is related by a 19-year-old black girl:

The experience which I have wanted to happen to me has finally happened. As a child I have always wanted to be able to curl and style hair, no matter what type of hair it may be. Now my wishes have come true. When this thought first occurred I was at the age of 9, I wanted to learn so badly that I took strings and placed them in a soda bottle then packed paper in to keep it from coming out. Some years later I was able to curl and style anything I wanted to. Now I am in the 11th grade and my main course is cosmetology. In the future, I plan to make myself known to everybody. (p. 99)

These and other experiences have been converted into data that have been subject to factor analysis, such as in the study of factors which seem to facilitate the experience and a taxonomy that has enabled us to compare the structure of various kinds of experiences with each other, for example, the relative frequency of experiences with the self, with the external world, and with human beings. Data are collected from children in the preschool years to octogenarians and from a wide variety of cultures and in a number of languages, specifically, at present, Hebrew, Spanish, and English.

This simple questionnaire is convincing as the most effective way to collect such data. It is anonymous; it permits time to the subject. He does not have to face another human being who might contribute to the distortion of the telling, as might occur in an interview. The writing activity encourages a more thorough recreation of the details of the experience. There are few reports that bear any of the marks of fakery, and these can readily be weeded out by trained observers.

Hadley Cantril (1950) complained, "No explanatory scheme so far offered gives an adequate account of man's experience" (p. 21). Since then Gendlin (1962) has presented an entirely reasonable conceptualization of the role of experience in theory, research, and application. Maslow (1971) without doubt made the greatest impact of all on the profession when he smashed the lock on the chamber, led his students into the area forbidden for 30 years, and discovered there the concept of the "peak experience." A number of psychologists who might otherwise be embarrassed to be in such company have successfully and comfortably utilized both hemispheres of this brain with no massive intracranial conflict: Hunt (1961) in *Intelligence and Experience* and Fiske and Maddi (1961) in *Functions of Varied Experience*.

IN SUMMARY

Exiled for perhaps two generations, psychologists primarily interested in human experience have prepared a quiet revolution, more likely a reasonable evolution that subjects experience to quantitative analysis and opens much, though not all, of this broadly defined area to the work of the humanistic scientist. Experience is seen as the subjective appreciation of stimuli, the awareness of undergoing of any stimulus or event, such as perceptions and sensations in simple or organized form of a specific response or organized form of states or conditions such as anxiety, emotion, or the self. Efforts to completely exclude internal states or experience from the subject matter of psychology are fated to impoverish the science and to delay the development of more rigorous methodology in the study of experience itself. Separate sciences of anthroponomy (Hunter, 1925) and phenomenology are the logical results of such divisiveness and would result only in a mutual deprivation. The proper study of psychology is man; the proper definition of psychology is *the science of behavior and experience.*

References

Angell, J. R. *Psychology: An introductory study of the structure and function of human consciousness* (4th ed. rev.). New York: Holt, 1908.

Averill, L. A. *Introductory psychology.* New York: Macmillan, 1943.

Baggett, R. L. *Behaviors that communicate understanding as evaluated by teenagers.* Unpublished doctoral dissertation, University of Florida, 1967.

Baldwin, J. M. *Handbook of psychology* (Vol. 1) (2nd ed. rev.). New York: Holt, 1890.

Boring, E. G. *A history of experimental psychology* (2nd ed.). New York: Appleton-Century-Crofts, 1950.

Boring, E. G., Langfield, H. S., & Weld, H. P. (Eds.). *Foundations of psychology.* New York: Wiley, 1948.

Cantril, H. *The "Why" of human experience.* New York: Macmillan, 1950.

Dunlap, K. *Elements of psychology.* St. Louis: Mosby, 1936.

English, H. B., & English, A. C. *A comprehensive dictionary of psychological and psychoanalytic terms: A guide to usage.* New York: McKay, 1958.

Eysenck, H. J., Arnold, W., & Meili, R. (Eds.). *Encyclopedia of psychology.* New York: Herder and Herder, 1972.

Fiske, D. W., & Maddi, S. R. *Functions of varied experience.* Homewood, Ill.: Dorsey, 1961.

Fuerst, R. E. *Turning point experiences.* Unpublished doctoral dissertation, University of Florida, 1965.

Gendlin, E. *Experiencing the creation of meaning: A philosophical and psychological approach to the subjective.* New York: Free Press, 1962.

Guilford, J. P. *General psychology.* New York: Van Nostrand, 1939.

Harriman, P. L. *The new dictionary of psychology.* New York: Philosophical Library, 1947.

Hayes, E. D. *A comparative study of the manhood experiences of black and white young adult males.* Unpublished doctoral dissertation, University of Florida, 1969.

Hebb, D. O. *A textbook of psychology* (2nd ed.). Philadelphia: Saunders, 1966.

Hill, W. F. *Psychology: Principles and problems.* Philadelphia: Lippincott, 1970.

Hunt, J. M. *Intelligence and experience.* New York: Ronald Press, 1961.

Hunter, W. S. General anthroponomy and its systematic problems. *American Journal of Psychology,* 1925, *36,* 286–302.

James, W. *Psychology.* New York: Holt, 1892.

Landsman, T. *Positive experience and the beautiful person.* Presidential Address, Southeastern Psychological Association, Roanoke, Va., 1968.

Lynch, S. *The intense human experience: Its relationship to openness and self concept.* Unpublished doctoral dissertation, University of Florida, 1968.

Maslow, A. H. *The farther reaches of human nature.* New York: Viking Press, 1971.

McDougall, W. *An introduction to social psychology.* Boston: Luce, 1921.

Morgan, C. T., & King, R. A. *An Introduction to psychology* (4th ed.). New York: McGraw-Hill, 1971.

Munn, N. L. *Psychology: The fundamentals of human adjustment* (2nd ed.). Boston: Houghton Mifflin, 1951.

Munn, N. L., Fernald, L. D., & Fernald, P. S. *Introduction to psychology* (3rd ed.). Boston: Houghton Mifflin, 1969.

Paul, R. D. *Experiences which facilitate personal fulfillment.* Unpublished doctoral dissertation, University of Florida, 1968.

Pennell, L. A. *The relationship of certain experiences to psychological adjustment in persons with spinal cord injury.* Unpublished doctoral dissertation, University of Florida, 1969.

Perrin, F. A. C., & Klein, D. B. *Psychology, its methods and principles.* New York: Holt, 1926.

Privette, P. G. *Factors associated with functioning which transcends modal behavior.* Unpublished doctoral dissertation, University of Florida, 1964.

Ruch, F. L., & Zimbardo, P. G. *Psychology and life* (8th ed.). New York:

Scott Foresman, 1971.

Smith, S. M. *Intense experiences of black and white female prisoners.* Unpublished doctoral dissertation, University of Florida, 1973.

Titchener, E. B. *Outline of psychology* (New ed.). New York: Macmillan, 1902.

Warren, H. C. (Ed.). *Dictionary of psychology.* Boston: Houghton Mifflin, 1934.

Warren, H. C. *Elements of human psychology.* Boston: Houghton Mifflin, 1922.

Watson, J. B. *Behavior: An introduction to comparative psychology.* New York: Holt, 1914.

Watson, J. B. *Behaviorism* (Rev. ed.). Chicago: University of Chicago Press, 1930.

Weatherhead, L. D. *Psychology and life.* Cincinnati: Abingdon, 1935.

Weld, H. P. *Psychology as science: Its problems and points of view.* New York: Holt, 1928.

Woodworth, R. S. *Psychology: A study of mental life.* New York: Holt, 1921.

Wilson, G. D. Experience. In H. H. Eysenck, W. Arnold, & R. Meili (Eds.), *Encyclopedia of psychology.* New York: Herder and Herder, 1972.

3

Ego Development and the Interpersonal Relationship

CLIFFORD H. SWENSEN

Not so very long ago Sidney Jourard wrote that "psychologists have exciting new vistas of relevance for their know-how and commitment . . . our task as psychologists will be, not to make man more like an automaton for those who would control him; but rather to explore *our own* possibilities, as men, and to explore ways to help *all* men discover their own potentialities and to enlarge their freedom from determiners that limit freedom, that scientific psychology has discovered" (1971, p. 188). Psychology is on the verge of developing a single, general paradigm, integrating all fields of psychology, that will contain and promote these ends and which will transcend the old three-section division of psychology into psychoanalysis, behaviorism, and humanistic psychology.

This new paradigm is developing out of research ranging across the broad realm of psychology, from the behavioristic and experimental to the phenomenological and clinical. The paradigm centers around the study of cognitive processes and research that outlines the course of cognitive development. This course of cognitive development traces a process that begins with simplicity and develops toward increased complexity and integration; that begins with a person being at the mercy of the environment and develops toward an ability to transcend and change the environment; that begins with complete self-centeredness and develops toward an ability to understand and share the feelings and experiences of other people; and that begins with an inability to relate to anyone and develops toward a capacity for deep and intimate relationships with others.

This emerging paradigm promises to transcend the dichotomies that have divided psychology, and in the process to usher in a psychology that is both empirically rigorous and which promotes the realization of the values which humanistic psychology has held to be fundamental: that the whole man is the basic unit in psychology, that man is purposeful and responsible for working out his own salvation "with fear and trembling." In this chapter I describe what I feel are the sources of this new paradigm for psychology, and I outline a model for studying the interpersonal relationship that incorporates it.

THE EMERGING IMPORTANCE OF COGNITIVE PROCESSES

It seems to me to be clear that there is emerging a general paradigm in psychology and that this paradigm centers around cognitive processes. My awareness of this development is not new. I had been familiar with Piaget's studies (e.g., 1948; 1970) of intellectual development, Kohlberg's research (e.g., 1968) on intellectual development, and O. J. Harvey's (e.g., 1963; 1966) studies of cognitive complexity. It occurred to me, vaguely, that this research might have some applicability to my own studies of interpersonal relations, but it did not occur to me how this general area of research might be directly applicable, nor did it occur to me that this research might be converging toward a general theoretical paradigm for all of psychology.

For many years I have been studying, doing research on, and writing about interpersonal relationships. It had seemed to me that to study the interpersonal relationship, you must study it at the level of the phenomenon, as is suggested by Ronald Laing (1962; 1969). That means that relationships must be studied at the level of the relationship. Relationships must vary along some dimensions. Many different lines of research (Swensen, 1973a) seemed to indicate that the dimensions along which relationships varied were the two dimensions of dominance-submission and interpersonal approach—interpersonal avoidance; or love-hate as Timothy Leary (1957) described it.

Further, it seemed to me that the kind of relationship two people produced must be the function of the kinds of people who were involved in the relationship. That is, a relationship is a function of the kinds of personality traits exhibited by the two people involved in the relationship. Because dominance-submission and approach-avoidance seemed to be the dimension along which relationships varied, it would appear that the kind of relationship that developed between two people should be a function of where these two people stood relative to each other on the personality dimension of dominance-submission and approach-avoidance. Some research on marriage relationships (Winch, 1958) had already provided what appeared to be some support for this position. Thus, using Leary's methods of measurement, I embarked on a series of studies designed to study the relationship between two people as a function of these two personality traits. This included both experimental and survey research (Swensen, 1967; Swensen & Nelson, 1967). Although this research produced some interesting results, it did not produce consistent results. I had the feeling that there was something in this area, but my research was clearly not getting directly at it. It then occurred to me that the personality of the participants in a relationship certainly does have a direct relationship to the kind of relationship that they develop, but that the personality variables I was studying were not the essential personality variables.

When Maslow studied self-actualizing people (1970) he

observed that self-actualizing people formed particular kinds of relationships with those people with whom they chose to be intimate. It occurred to me that perhaps the level of "self-actualization" of the people involved in a relationship would be related to the kind of relationship they developed. At the time this thought occurred to me I was preparing to spend a year at the University of Florida. Sidney Jourard very kindly lent me a class of his, in return for which I agreed to teach the class for a few meetings while he was away lecturing. I gave the members of this class a measure of self-actualization, Shostrom's Personal Orientation Inventory (1966), and picked out subjects who were high, medium, and low on self-actualization. I then used my own love scale (1973b) and an interview to measure their intimate relationships with two persons, the closest friend of the same sex and the closest friend of the opposite sex. I found clear differences among the three groups. The group that was low on the self-actualization measure had no relationships, or their relationships were broken or seriously conflicted. Most of this group had no current close relationships. The group that was medium on self-actualization had relationships, but their descriptions of these relationships were romanticized and stereotyped. Their relationships were practically perfect, as they described them, with no problems. The group that was the highest on self-actualization also had intimate relationships, but they described their relationships realistically. That is, they could describe the good characteristics of the relationships, but they also described the problems they had in those relationships.

These results suggested to me that actualization was worth exploring further as a personality variable of significance to interpersonal relations. Thus when I returned to Purdue I taught a seminar on humanistic psychology in which we devoted ourselves to discussing ways in which we might usefully measure various psychological variables that might reflect self-actualization. From this my class and I developed a series of areas to explore in an interview that could be scored for level of self-actualization. Using this interview outline, I interviewed a small group of married couples and obtained descriptions of their marriage relationships, which I related to their level of self-actualization. All of this group would probably be rated from medium to high on self-actualization. All could describe aspects of their marriage relationship that bothered them. However, the married couples that were lowest on self-actualization had conflicts that could best be described as "sibling rivalry" or as arguments over roles. The couples who were highest in self-actualization described their problems in terms of helping each other develop and grow. These two small pilot studies indicated to me that I was on the track of a very useful variable related to interpersonal relations, an indication that was further confirmed by the thesis research by a graduate student on marriage (Kemp, 1974).

Along about this time I became aware of the research of Jane Loevinger (1966) on ego development. The concept of self-actualization is a seminal one, but it has certain theoretical and psychometric problems. Loevinger, on the other hand, in developing her concept of ego development, has tied it in with many different strands of psychological research and has developed a very useful method, a sentence completion test (1970), for measuring it. I would like to briefly review some of the strands of thinking and research that are woven together into the concept of ego development, because I believe that the different sources of these strands suggest that psychology is moving toward a single paradigm.

In 1973 I published a book (Swensen, 1973a) surveying theories and research in interpersonal relations. In concluding that book I suggested that the study of interpersonal relations had not yet developed a single paradigm, but that when it did it would probably be a paradigm that derived from Harry Stack Sullivan's system (1953). From Harry Stack Sullivan's system, three other people, Sullivan, Grant, and Grant (1957) elaborated Harry Stack Sullivan's stages of development. These stages have been used to develop an interpersonal relations approach to changing the behavior of delinquents in growth-promoting directions (Palmer, 1971; Jesness, 1971). Research suggests that this approach to delinquents has an effect in predicted directions. In addition, the stages of self development described by Sullivan, Grant, and Grant appear to be quite similar to the five kinds of character found in an independent sociological study of character development in adolescents (Peck & Havighurst, 1960). Further, as Carson has pointed out, the development of Sullivan's self-system is essentially a process of cognitive learning that "pictures man as an information-processing, planful, decision-making animal" (1969, p. 82).

A second strand contributing to the concept of ego development derives from developmental psychology. Piaget has described the stages of moral development (1948) as well as intellectual development in the child. This Piagetian concept has been greatly expanded by Kohlberg (1968) into an extended concept of moral development, containing six stages. Kohlberg's concept of moral development has been applied to the study of the intellectual and moral development of college students (Perry, 1970). This study suggests that college students progress through three clearly definable stages: a conformist stage, in which they are primarily trying to learn the rules and facts from authority; a relativistic stage, in which they perceive a variety of rules and interpretations of facts, with each person free to choose his own interpretations; and a stage of commitment, in which the person consciously commits himself to a particular set of interpretations and values. The process of development of college students appears to be particularly concentrated in two of Kohlberg's six stages. These stages of moral and intellectual development are essentially stages of cognitive development.

A third strand of development issues from social psychology and the concept of cognitive complexity. Bieri describes the concept of cognitive complexity as standing at the junction of the converging streams of Piaget, Tolman, and Lewin in experimental psychology, and of ego psychology (1966). Harvey (1963; 1966) has described four systems, or stages, of cognitive complexity. His four stages are similar to the stages of self-development and moral development.

Finally, a change has been taking place within behavioristic, experimental psychology. Segal and Lachman (1972) point to the rapid development of cognitive psychology within experimental psychology and argue that the problems within the behavioristic S-R paradigm, coupled with developments within other areas of science, have led to a shift away from the old S-R paradigm toward the inclusion of concepts that were formerly rejected as mentalistic. They argue that this changes the basic conception of man within experimental psychology and that they "can say with assurance that deep conceptual changes in psychology have already occurred" (p. 53).

This approach to understanding behavior has even penetrated as far afield as theology, where it is now being used to develop a general theory of myth and symbol (Homans, 1975).

It should be added here that these stages of development, as described from these various points of view, show a certain similarity to Maslow's concept of a hierarchy of needs (1970), with higher-order needs emerging as lower needs are satisfied. This shift is also in the direction of the basic concepts held by humanistic psychology, including the concept of the self as being the central core of the person and the person tending toward higher degrees of order over the course of life (Buhler & Allen, 1972).

I have described these strands emerging from clinical psychology, developmental psychology, social psychology, experimental psychology, sociology, and theology for two reasons. One reason is to support my assertion that a single paradigm is in the process of being born in psychology. The second reason is as an introduction to Loevinger's concept of ego development, which seems to me to be the central personality variable in interpersonal relations.

THE CONCEPT OF EGO DEVELOPMENT

Loevinger (1966; 1970) sees her concept of ego development as encompassing but not being identical to moral development, character development, and cognitive development. Ego development is the "master" personality trait, which describes the stages of development of the ego or self-system and which organizes and integrates all other aspects of the personality. Several continua run through the stages of ego development from the least mature to the most mature. The person develops from the earliest stage, in which there is no cognitive differentiation, to the higher stages, in which there is extensive differentiation of persons, situations, objects, feelings, and actions. The person develops from no integration of his various needs, responsibilities, and relationships to a harmonious integration of the various forces in his life. The person develops from total self-centeredness to being able to understand and share the feelings, thoughts, needs, and experiences of other people. The person develops from being totally at the mercy of his environment to being able to have an effect on the environment. And the person develops from an inability to relate to other people to being able to relate deeply, intimately, and harmoniously with other people.

People pass through the stages of ego development in the same order. The tasks and problems of one stage must be met and satisfied before the person can move on to the next stage. Each stage is built on the previous stages, so that the perceptions, feelings, and behavior of each previous stage remain within the person.

Each stage of development is a cognitive stage, which characterizes the way a person sees and interprets the world, events, and other people. People at a particular stage of ego development describe and interpret events in terms that are appropriate to that stage.

Loevinger's stages of ego development are the following:

1. Presocial, in which the person is unable to distinguish himself from others. His interpersonal style is autistic. The person's behvior is motivated entirely by his immediate impulses. The person in this stage is unable to relate to other people. This stage is characteristic of newborn infants and severely regressed psychotics.

1a. Symbiotic, in which the person can distinguish himself from the environment, but does not sharply differentiate himself from other people. His behavior is still motivated largely by his immediate impulses. The interpersonal relations of this person are symbiotic. This stage is characteristic of infants prior to the development of speech and of regressed psychotics. When the infant develops the ability to speak, this stage comes to an end. With the development of speech, the person begins to develop the ability to have some control over his environment.

2. Impulsive, in which the control of impulses is lacking or is undependable. The person confirms his existence as being separate from others by the exercise of the will, which usually takes the form of negativism. In small children this is the stage in

which they begin to say "no" to suggestions made by their parents. The person in this stage is concerned with sexual and aggressive impulses. If the person in this stage recognizes rules that govern the behavior of people, it is primarily as a basis of punishment for the violation of rules, so that if he behaves in accordance with rules, it is to avoid punishment. Impulses are curbed primarily by immediate reward and punishment in the environment. This person sees events as being caused by magical processes. What is moral is what feels good. Other people are perceived primarily as sources of supply for his needs. His relationships with other people are dependent and exploitive.

DELTA is a self-protective or manipulative stage in which the person recognizes the existence of rules that govern the behavior of people, but perceives the rules as something to be obeyed for personal advantage. Loevinger originally labeled this stage as a "manipulative" stage, but subsequent investigation of these people led her to conclude that they manipulated people primarily for self-protection. They view the world as a kind of jungle in which each person is out for himself. Morality is purely a matter of expediency. What is bad is to get caught. In this stage there is a shift away from dependency on other people, because being dependent on other people puts a person at a disadvantage. This person's conscious preoccupation is with control and advantage, and to avoid being taken advantage of by other people. These persons tend to blame other people or circumstances for their problems. They see life as a kind of zero-sum game in which there are winners and losers, and they do not want to be losers. Their relationships with other people are primarily for exploitation and personal advantage. They relate to other people for what they can get out of the other people.

3. Conformist, in which the person has partially internalized the rules of society and feels that the roles are to be obeyed because they are the rules. The chief sanction for the transgression of rules is shame. This person's conscious preoccupation is with reputation, status, appearance, and adjustment. Statements about personal feelings are stereotyped, banal, and moralistic. People at this stage are concerned with how things are supposed to be done and in discussing their own behavior are likely to ask such questions as "Isn't that what anybody would have done in

that situation?" and "It's normal to feel like that, isn't it?" People in this stage are concerned with how they compare to other people and with the rules that govern various situations. They assume there are rules to cover every situation. They are disturbed by other people who do not follow the rules as they understand them. Other people are perceived in terms of stereotyped characteristics that are attributed to the groups they belong to, such as sex, age, race, or socioeconomic class. People in this stage do not sharply differentiate between the way things are and the way they should be. They relate to other people in rather stereotyped ways and describe relationships in terms of actions rather than in terms of feelings or needs of motivation. Interpersonal reciprocity occurs, but it is likely to occur because the rules prescribe that it should, rather than from any perception of the needs of the other person in the relationship. Trust occurs, but it is to a narrow in-group, whereas prejudice toward out-groups is common. Loevinger feels that most adults in most societies are in this stage.

4. Conscientious, in which morality is internalized, so that the person's own moral principles take precedence over the popularly accepted public rules. The sanction for transgression is guilt. The person's conscious preoccupation is with ideals, achievement, personal traits, and obligations as measured by the person's own internal standards rather than by external, publically accepted rules alone. This person is concerned with the internal origins of conduct. Self-criticism is characteristic of this stage and the development of self-criticism is part of the process of maturation from the conformist stage to the conscientious stage. People begin to move from the conformist stage toward the conscientious stage when they perceive conflicts in the rules. Some of their rules conflict with other rules, or they discover that their rules conflict with the rules of other people, or they discover situations in which the rules do not apply or do not work. Thus it becomes necessary to either deny their own experience or develop a more workable view of life.

The person at this stage is able to have a feeling for the feelings of other people and to understand other people in terms of their internal psychological processes, rather than in terms of whether they did or did not follow some set of rules. They are likely to be very concerned with the meaning of their own life and the meaning of life in general, and in the significance of their own behavior and the significance of the behavior of other people. They are able to see several possible acceptable ways of behaving in a situation. Rules are seen to have exceptions or to apply only to certain circumstances. Inner states of feeling and individual differences are described in vivid and differentiated terms. They feel guilty not so much when they have broken a rule as when they have hurt another person. Motives for behavior and the consequences of behavior are more important than rules. The way things are is clearly differentiated from the way things ought to be. This person strives for goals and is concerned with achieving goals, living up to ideals, and improving himself. Achievement is important, but is more a matter of meeting one's own inner standards than of winning social approval or a competition.

The person in this stage perceives interpersonal relations in terms of feelings, motives, needs, and personality characteristics rather than in terms of actions. Interpersonal relations become more vivid, intense, and meaningful. It is perhaps paradoxical that as the person becomes more sensitive to the deeper dimensions of interpersonal relations, he also becomes more aware of the conflicts, problems, and dissatisfactions that exist within his relationships with other people.

5. Autonomy, in which the chief moral issue for the person is the internal conflict both between conflicting duties, and between duties and personal needs. The conscious preoccupations of this stage are role differentiation, individuality, and self-fulfillment. The person at this level recognizes that there are some problems and conflicts in life that are perennial and apparently insoluble and has accepted that fact. Relationships with other people are seen as partly in conflict with achievement and also partly in conflict with the moralism and responsibility of the conscientious level. The moralism of lower stages is replaced by an awareness of inner conflict. At this stage the conflict is seen to be only partly internal. The person at the autonomous level recognizes that conflict is part of the human condition. Moral dichotomies are replaced by a feeling for the complexity of real people and real situations. There is a deepened respect for other people and a realization of the need of other people to find their

own way and to make their own mistakes. The striving for achievement of the conscientious stage is partially replaced by a striving for self-fulfillment. In acknowledging inner conflict, the person has come to accept the fact that not all problems are soluble. Inner conflict is not more characteristic of the autonomous person, but rather the autonomous person has the courage to acknowledge and cope with conflict. He tries to be realistic and objective about himself and other people.

This person's interpersonal relations are intense, and they include a recognition of interdependence with other people, but they also recognize the need of the other person for autonomy. There is a toleration for the other person's seeking different solutions to problems from one's own solution. There is a recognition of the need for the other person in the relationship to make his own mistakes. The autonomous person is willing to allow the other person in the relationship to be himself or herself.

6. Integrated, in which the person has reconciled conflicting demands. He has renounced the unattainable. This person has moved beyond tolerating individual differences toward cherishing individual differences and has moved beyond accurate role differentiation to an integrated identity. He has transcended conflict and reconciled the polarities. He has "put it all together." This person's interpersonal relations are characterized by promoting the growth and development of the people with whom he relates. This person relates to others in a manner described by Maslow as self-actualized.

If you recall the earlier description of the results of my pilot study of the interpersonal relationships of people at three different levels of self-actualization, they seem to fit some of the stages of ego development. You will recall that my group with low self-actualization had relationships that were either nonexistent, broken, or conflicted. These relationships would seem to fit the description for the kinds of relationships formed by people at the impulsive or self-protective stages of ego development. The subjects in the study were all college students, thus they were probably at the self-protective level. Probably few impulsive people get to college, or if they do get there, they fail to manage to remain long enough to take a second course in psychology. The people in my middle level of self-actualization described their relationships in phrases that are typical of the conformist stage. The group with the highest level of self actualization described their relationships in phrases that correspond to the conscientious level of ego development. I should add, parenthetically, that Loevinger has found that most college students seem to be in the conformist and the conscientious stages of ego development. Perry's (1970) research suggests that in college most students develop from the conformist stage to the conscientious stage.

My study of the relationship of married couples as a function of level of self-actualization also seems to fit these stages of ego development. My group that was low in self-actualization discussed their marriages in phrases that typify the conformist level of ego development, whereas the married couples with the highest level of self-actualization described their marriages in phrases that seem appropriate to the autonomous stage of ego development.

Thus ego development seems to be a personality variable that is a significant factor in the way people relate to each other. However, the concept of ego development appears to me to have an even broader significance. It seems to me that it provides a way of organizing theories, a way of relating theories to one another, and a way of selecting which theory to apply to a particular segment of interpersonal behavior.

The first three levels of ego development, especially the impulsive and the self-protective levels, are characterized by behavior that is determined primarily by reward and punishment. Reward and punishment are, of course, central to behavioristic theories of behavior. Therefore, it would appear that behavioristic theories of interpersonal behavior, such as exchange theory (Swensen, 1973a, ch. 8) and reinforcement theory (Swensen, 1973a, ch. 9) are particularly applicable to the interpersonal behavior of people at these stages of ego development.

Interpersonal relations at the conformist level of relationship are characterized by a concern for the rules people are supposed to follow. A concern for the rules, or a concern for who is supposed to do what, is the primary focus of role theory. Because most people in a society are at the conformist stage of ego development, a theory developed from a study of the people in general could be expected to be concerned with who is supposed to do what and should look very much like contemporary role theory, (Swensen, 1973a, Chaps. 12 and 13). From the point of view of ego development concepts, it is, therefore, not surprising that sociology has particularly tended to emphasize role theory.

Humanistic psychology has particularly tended to emphasize the fact that there is more to man than obtaining rewards, avoiding punishment, and behaving in accordance with the rules or role prescriptions of society. Humanistic theory has emphasized that man tends to grow through life and that this growth is toward self-fulfillment or self-actualization. However, growth and self-fulfillment do not become central concerns for the person until the later stages of ego development are reached.

The idea I am suggesting is that all the widely used theories of interpersonal behavior have some value. They are of use for explaining the interpersonal behavior of people at some stage of ego development, but only the more complex theories—which include the aspects of man that have been emphasized by humanistic psychologists—are broad enough to explain interpersonal behavior at all levels of ego development. Perhaps the chief shortcoming of humanistic psychological theory is that in order to get its point across it has overemphasized the self-actualization aspects of man and has therefore ignored or deemphasized reinforcement theories and role theories, which come closer to explaining the behavior of a large proportion of the population, who are motivated more by a desire to obtain reward and to follow the rules than by a desire to gain self-fulfillment. But when viewed from the perspective of ego development, the extant theories of interpersonal relations have something to contribute to the understanding of how people relate to each other and how the theories can be related to one another within the framework of ego development.

When we view the interpersonal relationship from the vantage point of ego development, some of the theoretical controversies within interpersonal relations appear to be resolved. Some of the controversies are only applicable to people in a particular stage of ego development, and other controversies could perhaps arise from studying people at different stages of ego development. For example, the extensive controversy over the relative importance of roles versus complementary needs in marital interaction (see Swensen, 1973, Chaps. 10 and 12), when viewed from the perspective of ego development, appears to be a function of studying people at two different levels of ego development. People in the conformist stage are quite concerned with roles and role performance, whereas people at the conscientious stage of ego development are more likely to be concerned with their own needs and the needs of their mate and with how the two sets of needs relate. The general conclusion that seems to have emerged from this controversy is that role theory is the more efficacious approach to marriage interaction (Tharp, 1963; Barry, 1970). However, it is difficult to see how two married people who are in the autonomous stage of ego development could get very concerned about who does the after-supper dishes or who pays the bills. For people in the autonomous stage specific role behaviors are matters of relative unimportance.

As a matter of fact, I have been doing research on the marriage relationships of older married couples, and the results I am obtaining indicate that roles are relatively unimportant to this group. These older married couples I am studying average 65 years of age with 38 years of marriage. They are quite different from the younger married couples that I have studied. These older people are quite explicit in describing what they like and what they do not like about their marriage relationship and about their spouses. They also have a rather clear idea of what their spouses do and do not like. They are quite unconcerned about roles in marriage. Many of these couples are lower middle class and include people working in factories and on construction. They are the sort of people who would be expected to be concerned with playing the proper role in marriage. And yet I have found it quite common among this group, when it is no longer financially necessary for both the husband and wife to work, for the wife to continue to work because she enjoys her job, and for the husband to stay at home and keep house because he would rather do that than continue to work at a job he does not enjoy. These couples seem to have grown beyond the conformist stage into what appears to me to be the autonomous stage. They are accepting of each other's foibles. They know what they do not like about each other, but they are no longer trying to change the other person. They are willing to let their spouse be himself or herself. Another interesting characteristic I have observed about these older people is that when there is a conflict between them, they tend to blame themselves rather than the other person for the conflict. Rather than saying "If he would just behave differently," they say, "If I had just handled the situation differently."

My experience with these older married couples fits a hypothesis Maslow suggested (1971). Maslow hypothesized that people should develop as they grew older, and therefore, older people should be relatively more self-actualized. This would mean that they would be more accepting of others, more accurate in their perception of others, and would be more likely to assume personal responsibility for what transpires in their relationships. This is precisely what I am finding in these older married couples. In terms of ego development theory, these couples are willing to allow their spouses to be themselves, which places them in the autonomous stage of ego development.

I might add that in presenting these ideas to a faculty colloquium at Purdue recently a faculty member who is engaged in training crisis-center volunteers remarked that the stages of ego development described very well the reactions to crisis-center training of volunteers. The volunteers who were at the self-protective level were dropped from training; the volunteers at the conformist level had some difficulties, but tended to change in the direction of the conscientious level; the conscientious level volunteers fit in very well, because they were able to relate well to the trainers, who seemed to also be at the conscientious level; and the volunteers at the autonomous level did well, but seemed to drop out after a period of time because of boredom.

THE PERSON-SITUATION INTERACTION

However, the ego or the self, at whatever stage of development, does not operate in a vacuum. The ego operates in an environment. Behavioristic psychology has tended to emphasize behavior as a function of the environment, to the exclusion of the organism. This trend perhaps reached its high point with Mischel's (1968) publication of *Personality and Assessment*. This stress on the situation as the primary determinant of behavior was in reaction to the failure of much of personality research to demonstrate a stable, significant relationship between personality traits and behavior over different kinds of situations. The beginning of this disenchantment may be traced to the studies of Hartshorne and May (1928) which demonstrated that children are not consistently honest in different kinds of situations. However, such recent studies as the Menninger studies of psychotherapy (Voth & Orth, 1973) have concluded that even in psychotherapy, in which the main goal is to change the personality, the primary change in behavior is a function of change in the environment.

The observation of the fact that the behavior of a person is not consistent over different situations, but that behavior does change as a function of a change in the situation, has suggested to some that there are no such entities as traits or personality characteristics located within people that predispose them to behave in certain ways regardless of the situation.

The view that a person's behavior is a function of the situation and not of the person is, of course, directly contradictory to the assertion of humanistic psychology that people are responsible and that people tend to behave in ways that lead toward self-development. The humanistic view that the self is the central core of the person and that the development of the self is the central concern of the person is diametrically opposed to the idea that behavior is a function of the situation. The behavioristic view either denies the existence of such an entity as a self or, at best, considers it an epiphenomenon.

However, when viewed from the perspective of ego development, this controversy is solved. People at the lower levels of ego development are, to a large extent, at the mercy of their environment. Even at the conformist level the person is motivated largely to obtain the approval of other people and to avoid the shame that could come from the disapproval of other people. Only at the higher levels of ego development does concern with the internal processes of the self and self-fulfillment become an observable factor in the behavior of people. Thus there is some truth to the behavioristic assertion that behavior is essentially a function of the situation. However, the larger truth is that people can and do develop beyond being determined by their circumstances.

Subsequent research has demonstrated that behavior is determined both by the person and the situation. Raush (1965) demonstrated, through the use of Markov chains, that a person's "traits" can remain constant from one situation to another and yet that person's behavior can change from one situation to another. This demonstration by Raush suggests that a person's behavior in a given situation is a function of the interaction between the person and the situation, rather than a function of either the person or the situation exclusively.

Reviews of the research on the person-situation interaction conclude that the largest proportion of variance in behavior is attributable to the person-situation interaction, rather than to the person alone or to the situation alone (Bowers, 1973; Endler, 1973; Argyle & Little, 1972). In a review of eleven studies, for example, Bowers found that a mean of 12.71% of the variance came from the person, 10.17% from the situation, and 20.77% from the interaction between the two.

Bowers further pointed out that persons and situations are not independent of one another. Persons affect situations, and situations affect persons. Clearly, situations affect persons, often in ways that permanently change the person. Personality research indicates that many personality characteristics are partially or mostly a function of exposure to certain kinds of experience (e.g., Cattell, 1957). Some of the research on character development (e.g., Peck & Havighurst, 1960) would suggest that the level of ego development is at least partially a function of experience.

But persons also affect situations in at least three ways. First, a person reacts to a situation in terms of how he perceives the situation. People do not react to situations, they react to their perceptions of situations. Therefore, a person's behavior in a situation is not a direct reaction to the situation, but rather to the person's perception of the situation. Second, people can choose which situation they will enter. Research on occupational choice, for example, shows that people with particular personality traits tend to gravitate toward certain kinds of jobs (e.g., Myers, 1962). Third, people may directly affect the situation and change it. For example, Raush's (1965) studies of aggressive and normal children demonstrated that aggressive children create chaotic situations, whereas normal children behave in ways that prevent situations from deteriorating.

Perhaps this argument was brought to an end by Mischel's acknowledgement (1973) that behavior is a function of the person and the situation. Further, Mischel suggests that the degree to which the person determines his behavior in a situation may be related to the situation itself. In a weak and ambiguous situation the person determines his behavior, but in a strong situation the situation dictates the behavior to the person. Thus in a strong situation, such as a fire in a building, most people would leave the building as rapidly as conditions permitted.Although, we must concede, even in this situation there might be some variation in individual behavior. An unusually brave or foolhardy person might remain behind to search the building for any people who might have been left behind. In a relatively weak situation, such as Sunday in a residential neighborhood, we would find people engaged in a wide variety of different activities.

Ego development theory suggests that, just as there is variation in the degree to which situations determine behavior depending on the strength of the situation, there is also variation in the extent to which different people are affected by situations. The behavior of people who are at the lower levels of ego development is determined to a large degree by the immediate situation. As we move up to the higher levels of ego development we find that peple are more able to transcend the situation. We would expect, in an experimental study, to find that people at, say, the self-protective level, would have much less variance in their behavior in a given situation than would people at the autonomous level of ego development. Studies of role relationships in marriage should show that people at higher levels of ego development should demonstrate a wider variance in role behaviors in marriage (or any other role-specified situation) than would people at the lower levels of ego development.

Thus it seems reasonable to hypothesize that not only is behavior a function of the interaction between the person and the situation, but that both situations and persons can vary along dimensions such that the interaction between the two will produce relatively more situation-determined behavior or more person-determined behavior. This is, of course, a testable hypothesis. It is also a hypothesis that transcends the dichotomy between the behavioristic assertion that the situation determines the behavior and the humanistic view that people are responsible.

A MODEL FOR
INTERPERSONAL RELATIONSHIPS

The course of both research and thinking indicates that behavior is a function of both the person and the situation. If we extrapolate this observation to the interpersonal situation, it follows that the interpersonal relationship is a function of the persons involved in the relationship and the situation within which the two people are interacting.

This observation that behavior is a function of the person and the situation is not exactly a new insight in psychology. In fact, it is an observation that has historically been made by many theorists (e.g., Ekehammar, 1974). However, one theorist whose formulation of the interaction has been particularly fruitful in stimulating research is Lewin, who postulated that behavior is a function of the person and the environment, or $B = f(P, E)$ (1951). I took Gerald Pascal's elaboration of this formula (1959) and applied it to clinical cases for planning therapy (Swensen, 1968). My elaboration resulted in a formula that stated that

$$\text{deviant behavior} = f \frac{\text{stress, maladaptive behavior and defenses}}{\text{support, adaptive behavior and defenses, strengths}}$$

I have found this formulation very useful in planning therapy and in teaching students how to understand what is going on with a person they are trying to help. I have found it to be a valuable heuristic device. Therefore, in developing a model for the interpersonal relationship, I have elaborated this model into a formula for the interpersonal relationship that simply adds one more person, so the model is

$$\text{relationship} = f \text{ (person}_1, \text{ person}_2) \text{ environment.}$$

Or, for simplicity's sake

$$R = f(P_1, P_2)E.$$

With this model it is possible to study the interpersonal relationship from the point of view of any theoretical bias. It may be studied from a rigorously behavioristic point of view, or it may be studied from a humanistic point of view. The implication of what I have written thus far is that, within the ego development point of view, this dichotomy can be transcended.

As the model is presented, there are three variables that are to be measured. The first variable is the relationship variable. This could be measured in many different ways. We might, if we wanted to confine ourselves to behavior observation, use Bales' interaction process analysis (1951) or Longabaugh's measure of resource exchange (1963). Or, if we wished to be humanistic we could use Shostrom's measure of the self-actualizing relationship (1966), Laing's interpersonal perception method (Laing, Phillipson and Lee, 1966), or my own love scale (1973b). Whatever measure we use, I think we should follow Laing's axiom that the phenomena to be studied should be measured at the level of the phenomenon, and therefore, the measure should be a measure of *relationship*. One suggestion I would make is that anyone embarking on a series of studies should use the same method of measuring the relationship throughout the studies, so that the effect of the person and environmental variables may be compared.

In measuring the personalities of the two people involved in the relationship, we could again use any useful measure of personality. However, the discussion up to this point clearly suggests that the primary personality variable to measure is the level of ego development. In fact, the thrust of my argument thus far is that if only one personality variable is measured, it should be the level of ego development.

However, I would suggest that there are additional personality variables that should also be measured. Earlier in the paper I pointed out that research on a variety of populations had consistently produced two personality dimensions that were related to the interpersonal relationship. These two dimensions were dominance-submission and approach-avoidance (Swensen, 1973a, ch. 7). If these dimensions repeatedly turn up in such diverse situations and relationships as problem-solving groups

(Borgatta, Cottrell & Mann, 1958; Carter, 1954), marriage (Foa, 1966; Winch, 1958), parent-child relationships (Schaefer, 1959), psychotherapy groups (Leary, 1957), and Navy combat information center teams (Schutz, 1958), then it would appear that there must be something of significance to these variables.

I am not sure what the precise contribution of these variables is to the interpersonal relationship. My experience with them in research, as I earlier described, suggests to me that they are not central in the sense that level of ego development is central. I am rather inclined at the present time to think of them as stylistic variables. For example, a person at the conformist level could be either dominant or submissive, or an extravert or an introvert. If he is a submissive introvert, he could be a conformist accountant working for some large corporation. If he is a dominant extravert he might be a successful, conformist life insurance salesman. The interpersonal relationships of our accountant and insurance salesman might appear to be quite different, and yet upon closer inspection we would find that both formed relationships, marriages let us say, that are rather stereotyped and that follow the basic rules for marriage in our society. The accountant and his wife might spend more time at home watching television, whereas the insurance salesman and his wife might spend a lot of time at the country club, but both marriages would be following rules, the one for the stay-at-home-television-watching set and the other the rules for the country-club set.

If my hypothesis is correct, then my model for the person within the interpersonal relationship would look something like a cone. A cone, because at the lower levels of ego development at the bottom of the cone there is much less differentiation and less cognitive complexity, whereas at the higher levels of ego development at the top of the cone there is extensive differentiation and integration. People at the higher levels of ego development have a much wider repertoire of cognitions, perceptions, and behavior available to them. A diagram of this is presented in Figure 1.

The final variable to be measured is the situation. Although behaviorists have emphasized the situation as the determining factor in behavior, they have not done much about it. Humanists have emphasized the person in behavior, thus they have tended

Figure 1. Diagram of the model of the person variables
in the interpersonal relationship.

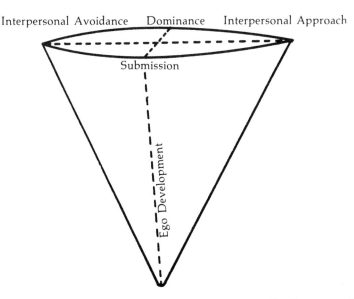

to ignore situational factors, and perhaps they can be forgiven for
having overlooked the measurement of this variable. This lack of
attention to the measurement of situation has been widely decried
(e.g., Frederiksen, 1972), but until recently, like the weather, no
one has done much about it.

One of the most successful schemes developed for measuring
the situation has been Holmes's (1973) scale for measuring stress.
Holmes's scale is a method for scaling the amount of stress
produced by various environmental events such as the death of a
spouse, a change in work responsibilities, and Christmas. His
research has demonstrated that as the amount of change within a
2-year time period increases the amount of physical and
emotional distress increases.

Stern (1970) developed a measure for assessing different
kinds of college environments. He found that college environments can be described by two dimensions, vocational versus intellectual and protective versus expressive. Perhaps more important from the humanistic point of view, he suggested that

environments can be generally ordered along one main dimension, anabolic versus catabolic. The anabolic stimulates the person towards self-enhancing growth, whereas the catabolic is antithetic to personal development. This dimension certainly owes something to Maslow's concept of the eupsychian, or growth-promoting environment (1971).

However, it seems to me that there must be more than one dimension to the environment. Given the choice of measuring just one dimension of the environment, I would opt for growth-promoting versus growth-inhibiting, or Stern's anabolic versus catabolic. In fact, I am willing to concede that this is probably *the* important environmental variable affecting the interpersonal relationship. But, as was the case with the personality variable in the model, it seems to me, nonetheless, that there must be more than one dimension to the environment. The approach that seems most promising to me is that of Warr and Knapper (1968), who have used the semantic differential (Osgood, Suci, & Tannenbaum, 1957) to measure a wide variety of situations and events, including such things as examination, wars, cities, and holidays. If you can measure Christmas and London, then surely you can measure anything in the environment.

Factor analysis of the semantic differential seems to usually come up with three dimensions: evaluation, potency, and activity. Potency includes such dichotomies as good versus bad and pleasant versus unpleasant. Perhaps this dimension will turn out to be approximately identical with anabolic versus catabolic. The potency dimension contains such dichotomies as strong versus weak and hard versus soft. The activity dimension contains dichotomies like fast versus slow and active versus passive.

CONCLUSION

In this chapter I have suggested that we are on the verge of developing a general paradigm in psychology that will transcend the division we have had among psychoanalysis, behaviorism, and humanistic psychology. I have suggested that this transcendence is emerging from the study of cognitive processes and is pointing toward a process of cognitive development that takes place over the life span of the person who develops from a largely environmentally determined being whose behavior is largely a function of the rewards and punishments in the immediate environment toward becoming a being who transcends his immediate environment and whose behavior is motivated by a desire for self-fulfillment.

In this context I have developed a model of the interpersonal relationship that is derived from Lewin, but which incorporates the concepts of ego development, the personality variables of dominance-submission and interpersonal approach-interpersonal avoidance, and the environmental variable of growth-promoting versus growth-inhibiting. The model is relationship = f (person$_1$, person$_2$) environment.

I have no illusions that I have contributed anything that is either brilliant or likely to be long-lived. I have found, however, that it is a heuristically useful model that incorporates the values of humanistic psychology.

With my students I have been using the model as the basis for a series of studies of the marriage relationship. In one study (Eskew, 1975) we found that the level of commitment between husband and wife in a marriage is significantly related to the number of marriage problems and to the love relationship. With higher levels of commitment there is more love expressed and there are fewer marriage problems.

In another study (Hilmo, 1975) we measured the impact of the birth of the first child on marriage. Previous research had found that the birth of the first child creates more problems in marriages (Ryder, 1973), but that couples also report that there is a greater closeness between husband and wife after the birth of the first child (Russell, 1974). Our study showed that the love relationship between husband and wife stays the same, or perhaps increases a little after the birth of the first child, but that the number of problems in the marriage also increases.

These two studies are cited merely to indicate that I am finding my paradigm quite useful in designing research. I am also now using it clinically to assess and develop therapy approaches for the interpersonal relationships of people who come to the clinic for help. No doubt there is a certain amount of "Hawthorne effect" in all of this. No doubt, research and therapeutic success owes something to the intitial enthusiasm of the people involved rather than to the efficacy of the model. And no doubt, things will become more complicated as we progress. Whatever develops in the future, I am convinced that, as Maslow observed shortly before he died, "we are on the edge of a new leap into correlating our subjective lives with external objective indicators" (1971, p. 11).

References

Argyle, M., & Little, B. R. Do personality traits apply to social behavior? *Journal for the Theory of Social Behavior*, 1972, 2, 1−36.

Bales, R. F. *Interaction process analysis: A method for the study of small groups.* Reading, Mass.: Addison-Wesley, 1951.

Barry, W. A. Marriage research and conflict: An integrative review. *Psychological Bulletin.* 1970, 73, 41−54.

Bieri, J. Cognitive complexity and personality development. In O. J. Harvey (Ed.), *Experience; structure and adaptibility.* New York: Springer, 1966.

Borgatta, E. F., Cottrell, L. S., & Mann, J. M. The spectrum of individual interaction characteristics: An interdimensional analysis. *Psychological Reports*, 1958, 4, 279−319.

Bowers, K. S. Situationism in psychology: An analysis and a critique. *Psychological Review*, 1973, 80, 307−336.

Buhler, C., & Allen, M. *Introduction to humanistic psychology.* Monterey, Ca.: Brooks/Cole, 1972.

Carter, L. F. Evaluating the performance of individuals as members of small groups. *Personnel Psychology*, 1954, 7, 477−484.

Carson, R. C. *Interaction concepts of personality.* Chicago: Aldine, 1969.

Cattell, R. B. *Personality and motivation: Structure and measurement.* Yonkers-on-Hudson, N.Y.: World Book, 1957.

Ekehammar, B. Interactionism in personality from a historical perspective. *Psychological Bulletin*, 1974, 81, 1026−1048.

Endler, N. S. The person versus the situation—a pseudo issue? A response to Alker. *Journal of Personality*, 1973, 41, 287−303.

Eskew, R. W. *Factors in the marriages of older pre- and post-retirement couples.* Unpublished master's thesis, Purdue University, 1975.

Foa, U. G. Perception of behavior in reciprocal roles: The ringex model. *Psychological Monographs; General and Applied*, 1966, *80*(15, Whole No. 623).

Frederiksen, N. Toward a taxonomy of situations. *American Psychologist*, 1972, *27*, 114—123.

Hartshorne, H., & May, M. A. *Studies in the nature of character* (Vol. 1), *Studies in deceit* (Book one). New York: Macmillan, 1928.

Harvey, O. J. (Ed.). *Motivation and social interaction: Cognitive determinants*. New York: Ronald Press, 1963.

Harvey, O. J. (Ed.). *Experience; structure and adaptability*. New York: Springer, 1966.

Hilmo, J. A. *Transition to parenthood—planned and unplanned*. Unpublished master's thesis, Purdue University, 1975.

Homans, P. Psychology and hermeneutics: An exploration of basic issues and resources. *Journal of Religion*, 1975, *55*, 327—347.

Holmes, T. H.,& Masuda, M. Life change and illness susceptibility. In J. P. Scott & E. C. Senay (Eds.), *Separation and depression*. Washington, D.C.: American Association for the Advancement of Science, No. 94, 1973.

Jesness, C. F. The Preston typology study: An experiment with differential treatment in an institution. *Journal of Research in Crime and Delinquency*, 1971, *8*, 38—52.

Jourard, S. M. *Self-disclosure: An experimental analysis of the transparent self*. New York: Wiley-Interscience, 1971.

Kemp, T. E. *The two-student marriage: An emerging non-traditional family form*. Unpublished master's thesis, Purdue University, 1974.

Kohlberg, L. Moral development. In D. L. Sills (Ed.), *Encyclopedia of the Social Sciences*. New York: Crowell, Collier, and Macmillan, 1968.

Laing, R. D. *The self and others: Further studies in sanity and madness*. Chicago: Quadrangle Press, 1962.

Laing, R. D. *The divided self*. New York: Pantheon, 1969.

Laing, R. D., Phillipson, H., & Lee, A. R. *Interpersonal perception*. New York: Springer, 1966.

Leary, T. *Interpersonal diagnosis of personality: A functional theory and methodology for personality evaluation*. New York: Ronald Press, 1957.

Lewin, K. *Field theory in social science: Selected theoretical papers* (1st ed.). New York: Harper & Bros., 1951.

Loevinger, J. The meaning and measurement of ego development. *American Psychologist*, 1966, *21*, 195—206.

Loevinger, J., Wessler, R., & Redmore, C. *Measuring ego development* (2 vols.). San Francisco: Josey-Bass, 1970.

Longabaugh, R. A category system for coding interpersonal behavior as social exchange. *Sociometry*, 1963, *26*, 319—344.

Maslow, A. H. *Motivation and personality* (2nd ed.). New York: Harper & Row, 1970.

Maslow, A. H. *The farther reaches of human nature.* New York: Viking Press, 1971.

Mischel, W. *Personality and assessment.* New York: Wiley, 1968.

Mischel, W. Toward a cognitive social learning reconceptualization of personality. *Psychological Review*, 1973, *80*, 252–283.

Myers, I. B. *The Myers-Briggs type indicator.* Princeton, N. J.: Educational Testing Service, 1962.

Osgood, C. E., Suci, G. J., & Tannenbaum, P. H. *The measurement of meaning.* Urbana, Ill.: University of Illinois Press, 1957.

Palmer, T. B. California's community treatment program for delinquent adolescents. *Journal of Crime and Delinquency*, 1971, *8*, 74–92.

Pascal, G. R. *Behavioral change in the clinic: A systematic approach.* New York: Grune & Stratton, 1959.

Peck, R. F., & Havighurst, R. J. *The psychology of character development.* New York: Wiley, 1960.

Perry, W. G., Jr. *Forms of intellectual and ethical development in the college years: A scheme.* New York: Holt, Rinehart & Winston, 1970.

Piaget, J. *The moral judgment of the child.* Glencoe, Ill.: Free Press, 1948.

Piaget, J. *Structuralism.* New York: Basic Books, 1970.

Raush, H. L. Interaction sequences. *Journal of Personality and Social Psychology*, 1965, *2*, 487–499.

Russell, C. S. Transition to parenthood: Problems and gratifications. *Journal of Marriage and the Family*, 1974, *36*, 294–301.

Ryder, R. G. Longitudinal data relating marriage satisfaction and having a child. *Journal of Marriage and the Family*, 1973, *35*, 604–606.

Schaefer, E. S. A circumplex model for maternal behavior. *Journal of Abnormal and Social Psychology*, 1959, *59*, 226–235.

Schutz, W. C. *FIRO: A three-dimensional theory of interpersonal behavior.* New York: Holt, Rinehart & Winston, 1958.

Segal, E. M., & Lachman, R. Complex behavior or higher mental process: Is there a paradigm shift? *American Psychologist*, 1972, *27*, 46–55.

Shostrom, E. L. *Personal orientation inventory.* San Diego: Educational and Industrial Testing Service, 1966.

Stern, G. G. *People in context: Measuring person-environment congruence in education and industry.* New York: Wiley, 1970.

Sullivan, C., Grant, M. Q., & Grant, J. D. The development of interpersonal maturity: Applications to delinquency. *Psychiatry*, 1957, *20*, 373–385.

Sullivan, H. S. *The interpersonal theory of psychiatry.* New York: Norton, 1953.

Swensen, C. H. Psychotherapy as a special case of dyadic interaction: Some suggestions for theory and research. *Psychotherapy; Theory, Research and Practice,* 1967, *4,* 7−13.

Swensen, C. H. *An approach to case conceptualization.* Boston: Houghton-Mifflin, 1968.

Swensen, C. H. *Introduction to interpersonal relations.* Glenview, Ill.: Scott, Foresman, 1973a.

Swensen, C. H. Scale of feelings and behavior of love. In J. W. Pfeiffer & J. E. Jones (Eds.), *The 1973 handbook for group facilitators.* Iowa City, Ia.: University Associates, 1973b.

Swensen, C. H., & Nelson, D. *Interpersonal interaction as a function of attitude and personality.* Paper read at Midwestern Psychological Association, Chicago, 1967.

Tharp, R. G. Psychological patterning in marriage. *Psychological Bulletin,* 1963, *60,* 97−117.

Voth, H. M., & Orth, M. H. *Psychotherapy and the role of the environment.* New York: Behavioral Publications, 1973.

Warr, P. B., & Knapper, C. *The perception of people and events.* New York: Wiley, 1968.

Winch, R. F. *Mate-selection: A study of complementary needs.* New York: Harper & Row, 1958.

II

Philosophical
Frontiers

4

Humanistic Psychology: An Attempt to Define Human Nature

ELIZABETH LÉONIE SIMPSON

*W*hat is the definition of human nature? In many forms, that self-centered question has existed since the dawn of consciousness. Past answers have been partial, limited, and contradictory; nor are they produced lightly or uniformly today. "Human being" is not an easy abstraction, reducible in spritual terms to beliefs, in physical terms to nerve cells, or in psychological ones to conflicting mental or personality elements. These two words are dense, obscured by thickets of subjectivity. Their meaning varies ethically, politically, religiously, scientifically, as many ways as there are areas of human endeavor. To this lively disarray, humanistic psychologists have added a definitional vision which generally underlies the field and provides silent, taken-for-granted assumptions for clinical, philosophical, or scientific foundations.[1]

As a field of inquiry demarked in the 1960s, humanistic psychology exists as a validation of the Delphic oracle's advice to "know thyself."It provides approaches to understanding and defining the meaning of humanity for the individual. The nature of this definition is deeply important, for, as John Mann (1963) has pointed out, "other than psychology there is no other scientific discipline equipped to undertake the task of extending human limitations" (p. 274). The task, in humanistic psychology, is not merely the descriptive one of defining "social normality" and how to be that way, but also how to develop beyond it, to make ourselves the shapers of our being and our fate. The search is for personal meaning in the perceived universe: the task, the development of the total composite that is possible, the evolving, phenomenal self.

Through the understanding of ourselves grounded on our growth as whole entities within the unifying, integrating sweep of experience, we learn new assessments of the possible. How far we have come from the common definition of the 1940s of mental health as "freedom from anxiety" and the simple belief that the therapist's task was only to help the client to do better whatever he wished to do! Today our motivation is toward consciousness as a fusion of the objective and the subjective. It is toward meaning, toward the understanding of our lives and our universe. It is not the surcease of tension which, in many forms, we all utilize and enjoy. Unlike Baudelaire's condemned women, we are not "great haters of the real, of all that is not dreams." Meaning entails a convergence of the real and the dream, the longing for essence, existence, awareness and not, as the poet cries, for *The Abyss*, the "nothingness where all our senses cease" and he longs to shed "numbers and entities."

Human life is a labyrinth plotted by human perceptions and hopes, and so designed and destined to be deciphered by them. Developing a unified world view requires the integration of public knowledge and private experience, the scientific study of commonality, as well as the unique, personal experience of events. As early as 1939, when Kurt Goldstein wrote of the need for self-actualization experienced by the healthy, whole person, he went far beyond the definition of humanness in physical terms. But 25 years later, and even more recently, commonly used books in the field still generally referred to the origin of modern psychology as the establishment of Wundt's laboratory in 1897, where the body was studied as a biological organism. Typically, these works had no reference to humanistic psychology as such.[2]

In a steadfast movement apart from the main stream of academic psychology, Goldstein's work on what was knowable and desired by healthy persons was developed by others. One of these was Abraham Maslow (1954) who wrote one of the basic works in the field of delineating the relationship between motivation and personality. The experience of the self, the fulfillment of needs, and the search for meaning and personal growth became scientific and philosophical bases for the definition of human nature and the possibility of change. As Jourard (1968) wrote:

I know I am ready to grow when I experience some dissonance between my beliefs, concepts, and expectations of the world, and my perceptions of the world, I am also ready to grow when I experience boredom, despair, depression, anxiety or guilt. These emotions inform me that my goals and projects have lost meaning for me (p. 13).

In the study of human nature feeling and intellect are inseparable. Emotion represents meaning experienced within a person's life. Humanistic psychology has drawn heavily on philosophical thinking here, especially from Tillich and Kierkegaard. During this century Paul Tillich (1952) has described the anxiety caused by meaninglessness from the loss of the conscious experience of one's significance. Kierkegaard, the mid-nineteenth century founder of existentialism, wrote of the fear of nothingness. "He . . . who has learned . . . to be anxious has learned the most important thing." Lack of significance and of meaning leads to confusion and to apathy. Repeatedly, personal meaning has been described as a defining dimension of human existence. Individual meaning shapes how knowledge is made functional for each person. Meaning and being, including choice of attitude and action, are central to the understanding of the human self. Within these concepts others emerged: will and intentionality, guilt, and creative struggle, the ethic of conscious involvement toward growth and development, and the striving of the whole person to become the "best" himself or herself.[3]

The question has not been simply to define ideal personality, but to explore options as to what can be known and experienced by humans, and how new competencies lead to further development and involvement when they are chosen. The process and result of choosing vary, but choosing as commitment is a consistent characteristic of the individual seeking fulfillment, the "whole person engaged in the process of becoming the best that he can become" (Richards & Welch, 1973, p. 10).

Bugental (1967), describing the challenge which is being human, refused parallels between human functioning and that of other species. Rejecting the habits of conventional science, he felt that meaning and subjective, internal happenings were more important than the methods of objectivity in studying humans and that our concern should be with the unique, exceptional, and unpredicted as opposed to the "regular, universal, and conforming" (p. 10). The choice described is extensive. It is between possibility and actuality, between the future and the ideal, and between the present and the real—in short, between philosophy and science, between aspiration and the present human condition. It is in the complex combination of all of these factors that the nature of humanistic psychology develops.

A comprehensive conception of "humanness" would have to include two environments: the external one as well as the inner world of memories, thoughts, desires, and feelings. It would have to include both the public knowledge of science and private, personal, subjective, individual experience. The commonalities of generalized knowledge and principles with other events and entities are described by science. This process, founded on respect for provable truth, is a means to an end: the survival of the individual and, beyond that, the greater development of persons as separate and unique (Brain, 1966).

THE HISTORY OF
HUMANISTIC PSYCHOLOGY

Derived from philosophy and the humanities, psychology has developed into two sciences: one of behavior and one of consciousness. Four well-defined periods are discernible: the first period, beginning between 1900 and World War I and including the experimental psychology of William Wundt, was the breaking away from thinking that was largely philosophical, deductive, and speculative to the accumulation of facts that were based on experience and induction; during the second period, between the two world wars, behaviorism and Gestalt psychology emerged; subsequent to World War II psychology was recognized as a natural science of behavior; during the more recent fourth period, including the late 1950s, and 1960s, the humanistic and existential movements came together to begin what has been considered a "tangential reaction" (Giorgi, 1970, p. 45). This newly-shaped "third force" was clearly differentiated from the earlier forces of behaviorism and psychoanalysis.

Since that time the existential, humanistic movement has drawn its involved participants from many disciplines besides those of clinical and social psychology, anthropology, and philosophy, from which it began. Appropriately, Giorgi (1970) uses the German term *Geisteswissenschaften*, meaning the "sciences of the mind, of culture or of the spirit" (p. 53). This is indeed a very human holy trinity! He suggests that psychology should be considered a human, rather than a natural, science since human:

implies that we hope to consider as subject matter any activity or experience that man is capable of, and it also has the more specific connotation that there will be an emphasis on especially those activities that differentiate man from the rest of nature or from other types of living creatures (p. 99).

Human research is not neutral, and all facts are interpreted facts. "Psychology is essentially an inter-subjective science" (p. 190). With Charlotte Buhler, (Buhler & Massarik, 1968), Giorgi would agree that the criterion of being human is not having a human body, but, rather, interacting interpersonally, person-to-object, and person-to-spirit. It is searching for meaning and the building of identity within a culture.

Giorgi goes on to suggest three presuppositions for psychology as a human science: (a) fidelity to the phenomenon of humans as persons; (b) concern for uniquely human phenomena, and (c) the primacy of human relationships, as opposed to independent units of entities. Because our subject matter is the human as a person, the natural sciences techniques are inappropriate when they are "empirical, positivistic, reductionistic, objective, analytic, quantitative, deterministic, concerned with prediction and largely operating within the genetic bias and the assumptions of the independent observer"(p. 204). He believes that human sciences, on the other hand, are simply empirical and positive, affirming reality in their fidelity to phenomena as they appear.

Giorgi's beliefs are interesting and useful ones. Human beings always utilize engaged attitudes in their search for knowledge, and the acknowledgment of this perspective may be more honest and accurate than the pretense of objectivity and impersonality and faith in mathematical precision. "Real" science is more than the collection of precise, quantitative, logicodeductive, verifiable natural laws. Should it also include the study of what is said, thought, and felt, as well as done?

Much of this point of view is not new. Maslow (1965), for example, believed that the human being could be studied only as an irreducible unit whose data could not be generalized or abstracted. It follows from this view that: "Each man's task is to become the best himself. Joe Doakes must . . . become the best Joe Doakes in the world. This he can do, and only this is necessary or possible. Here he has no competitors (pp. 32−33). Allport (1955), too, was concerned with the delineation of idiographic laws, predictions about an individual case, rather than nomothetic laws about a class of cases. Three years before Giorgi's work, Watson (1967) pointed out that psychology did not have a paradigm that provided for the field of study a comprehensive, theoretical structure with integrating force. The scope of the contrasting concepts he presented was great. He included, for example, conscious versus unconscious mentalism, contentual objectivism versus subjectivism, determinism versus indeterminism, induction versus deduction, physiochemical mechanism versus vitalism, monism versus dualism, quantitative versus qualitative, rationalism versus irrationalism, and more.

Within this wide range have appeared the major emphases of humanistic psychology: a concept of human nature that accounts for the healthy unity of personality, self-determination, and the primacy of self, as well as the belief in values of creativity, self-actualization and fulfillment, and the idea that conscious processes offer valid data for scientific investigation of human essence (Severin, 1963).

Human beings, added Bugental (1963), are a process that supercedes the sum of part functions; they can be understood only as whole individuals centered in relationships, although not as group members. He described eight parameters of psychology which he believed the humanists were challenging:

1. The model of humanness as a composite of part functions,

2. The model of scientific knowledge taken from physics,

3. The model of practitioner taken from medicine,

4. Graduate training, which does not include research and practice,

5. The criterion of statistical frequency as a demonstration of truth,

6. The misbelief that research actually precedes practice,

7. The myth of need for clinical teams when what is required is simply an authentic encounter between human beings, and

8. That diagnosis is basic to treatment when what the therapist needs is knowledge of, not about, the client.

Two textbooks helped to summarize the field and extend these observations, together with the theoretical and clinical work of others (Rogers, 1955/1956; Combs & Snygg, 1959), into a humanistic psychology.The first of these works, now out of print, was Gale's (1969) *Developmental Behavior: A Humanistic Approach*, which contained a detailed and comprehensive description of human qualities from this point of view. The second (Buhler & Allen, 1972) set forth the task, clearly and simply, as the exploration of the behavioral characteristics and emotional dynamics of full and healthy living. Centering on experience and its meaning to the creative, valuing, self-realizing individual, the assumption is basic that to each person belong both the freedom and the responsibility for choosing his actions by himself, with others, or as a member of social groups. This exploration leads to the rejection of a mechanistic and reductive view of human life.

But choice and responsibility are not seen as simple tasks; the appalling enormity of this freedom was expressed by Kierkegaard when he wrote:

I experience dread in the dizziness of my freedom, and my choice is made in fear and trembling.

Out of a basic description of full and healthy living came one of the mature personality with an objective perception of the self and reality, including the acceptance of personal limitations. The mature person has the ability to give and receive affection, the capacity for creative self-fulfillment, a sense of responsibility for his or her own actions, and a unifying philosophy of life. Within that philosophy lies the origin of intentionality, wanting to live for something, for an objective that signifies life's meaning. Buhler (Buhler & Massarik, 1968) described four basic tendencies that human beings have toward the fulfillment of these objectives: (a) the satisfaction of basic needs, (b) a self-limiting adaptation, (c) a creative expansion, and (d) the maintenance or upholding of internal order. She saw the individual, consciously or unconsciously, as goal-directed throughout the life-cycle of growth, homeostasis, and decay, beset by a dualism of purposes that included both comfort and accomplishment. Goal-setting was a "natural unit of behavior" (p. 89), comparable to the gene as the unit of biological development.

Buhler went on to describe the psychophysical system that determines behavior, experience, and performance. This system is determined by five major factors: by the sequential order of growth and decline, individual endowment and congenital qualities, environmental influences on the use of potentialities, broader influences of the social system and cultural ideology, and the integrative system of personality. In attempting to account for these factors she went beyond descriptions to causality in ways that such theorists as Carl Rogers did not. In an early account, which has become standardized, Rogers (1955/1956) wrote that humanness is a process of becoming, of achieving worth and dignity through the development of potentialities. This process is accompanied by self-actualization, becoming what one can be, by creative adaptation, and by the use of new perceptions and new knowledge that transcend and outdate the old.

Roger's description is of the paramount values that underlie the proper definition of the human place in the universe. No science of the person can avoid the study of values and, since Rogers, many humanists have delineated certain values as indispensable to human development. Maslow (1971) described the values of creativeness, spontaneity, courage, and integration as growth-fostering. Included often are the existential values that serve to prevent alienation from sources of power and purpose (Bugental, 1965). These are wholeness, rootedness, identity, meaningfulness, and relatedness.

Like other aspects of human personality, the determinants of a personal hierarchy of values include such biological factors as age and genes, as well as such social ones as environmental responses to goal-setting or emotional dynamics displayed in behavior. Humanness cannot be understood without the recognition of values manifest in behavior and why they are chosen, "in the act of valuing consciousness and behavior become united" (May, 1967, p. 220). Stanley Krippner (1974) has gone even farther to suggest that perhaps the greatest contribution made by humanistic psychology is that science of the person cannot avoid values. "Valuing is creating," wrote the philosopher Nietzsche, "Hear it, ye creative ones! Without valuation the nut of existence is hollow."

HUMANISTIC PSYCHOLOGY TODAY

By 1975, thirteen years after the foundation of the Association for Humanistic Psychology,[4] humanistic psychology has been widely and variously experienced in public conferences and in the media. At that time the "new psychology" and its specialized vision of human nature were described in the *Los Angeles Times* as a means of "expanding man's awareness . . . (enhancing) creativity, health, learning, problem-solving and (the production of) . . . intrinsically rewarding ecstatic experiences" (Hoover, 1975, p. 1). The field was its concepts:

1. Individuality (defined as complexity, richness, and the power of mind and consciousness),

2. Holism of mind, body, and feelings (particularly as emphasized in medicine, education, and sports),

3. Subjectivity as well as objectivity,

4. Growth, self-actualization, self-transcendence as innate human characteristics,

5. Concern for the will and responsibility for oneself,

6. Use of energy flows and the natural ability of the body to balance itself, and, lastly,

7. The spiritual dimension which, as transpersonal psychology, many see as the psychology in the future.[5]

As attractive and comprehensive as this list is, it still neglects an important and enriching aspect of contemporary humanistic psychology: the responsibility not only for oneself and one's own development, but also for the amelioration of the lives of others! This responsibility includes the promotion of human welfare through an ideal of existence that is functional and can be worked for, consciously and deliberately, because its aims are achievable by human effort.

To be fully human means, as an adult, to have concerns that extend beyond the self, family, and the nation to all of humankind. It is to be in process, not to have arrived at an ideal state. Individual acts are constituent elements in the development of the social whole (Shklar, 1973). We need to know more about the effects of the external world, the social settings in which these individual changes in inner life take place, for our cultures may provide (or be lacking in) the nutrients necessary for development. The growth of the self does not occur in separation from others, apart from, and yet a part of, them. As Teilhard de Chardin (1965) wrote, projection of the evolutionary future gives the lie to radical individualism. Only in union with others, not in isolation, is self-fulfillment found, and that union, he believed, continued in conscious existence after death.

This concern with social issues is an emerging force in humanistic psychology. Our new knowledge can be put to work as wisdom in the service of humankind; that self-knowledge may be the basis for social action that aids in the development of others, of many or all, as well as in the development of the self.

Perhaps the time has come to emphasize the social determinants of development we can affect and change, and the inter-relationship of social values with access to individual freedom.

Does this possibility seem improbably utopian? There are many recent examples to show how this new perspective is growing.

A. Jerry Rubin (1976), head of the Yippies (Youth International Party) and, as a member of the Chicago Seven, one of the most visible activists during the 1960s, has recently elaborated on this theme. He predicts that a political movement, directly related to basic needs, will arise to implement the new consciousness. Based on human equality, it will put into practice new knowledge about body, mind, and spirit. Responsibility for each other will be a major value and goal of life seen as experience, rather than material possessions. Revolution, he writes, is an evolutionary process: "*I* am also a process. My personal growth and your personal growth match the growth of mass consciousness" (p. 5). Rubin believes that the fusion of the two movements, consciousness and politics, will politicize the growth movement, and provide a spiritual and psychological base for politics. This is a clear, if simplified, statement of the relationship between personal and social development.

B. In reporting issues raised at the annual Association of Humanistic Psychology meeting in Estes Park, David Welch (1975) challenged the assumption that more is always better, and that "openness, honesty, authenticity, and self-disclosure are best maximized" (p. 11). He went on to suggest that humanistic psychologists must come down off the mountain top because they are least effective in touching the lives of middle and poor America. "We must involve ourselves in the concerns of our routine existence and . . . it is in that involvement that larger social concerns can be met and challenged" (p. 11). Our concern should be less with our higher nature and consciousness than with the solution of everyday, existential problems: "Surely, being a humanist, carries with it an obligation to work for human rights, a sane economy, a whole environment, and a community that promotes the opportunity for optional well-being of all of us" (p. 11).

C. As another example, therapy has been seen as an agent for social change because it involves the reeducation of citizens or group members. Intervention on the therapist's part, which changes the behavior of individuals, can act as a reformation of inhibiting or repressive social structures (Bugental, 1971).

D. Increasingly, the integration between the development of the self and the social person has been described. Mario Fantini (1975), writing about the value of "socialized caring," emphasized the environmental effects. There is, he believes, a "carefully orchestrated sequence from nursery through adulthood that enables each person to assume direct responsibility in helping to promote conditions of social justice, of helping fellow-humans achieve dignity and worth" (p. 15).

E. Stanley Krippner (1974), in his Association for Humanistic Psychology presidential address, suggested that psychology could not justify dubious social practices based on incomplete or biased data. He pointed out that racism was bolstered by the use of Binet tests standardized on predominantly white and middle-class samples of the American population, but that ethnic and social class differences disappeared with pretraining in concept-formation. He also pointed out that child abuse was fostered by the use of drugs to prevent hyperkinetic activity or devices to prevent thumb-sucking. As a group, psychologists, including Freud, have stereotyped females as passive and tractable, and, until the 1970s, both the American Psychological Association and the American Psychiatric Association continued to associate homosexuality with mental illness. Krippner concluded his account of the negative impact of psychology with such a large number of examples that it would seem impossible for anyone to believe that psychology in practice is, or can be, separate from social ideology and issues.

F. In 1973, Will McWhinney, a professor of organizational behavior at the University of California at Los Angeles, published a model suggestion for social redesign for what he called *phenomenarchies*. These are communal societies with a form of open organization within which a life could take a variety of paths, depending on the range of human needs. Within this structure, working life would be integrated with nonworking life, and varying goals might be achieved in a network structure that connects the individual's needs and expectations. Employment would be by community contract; the concept of employment as opposed to unemployment would be eliminated. The result would be the redistribution of time based on needs for production, for community services, for family, and for personal concerns. The goal would be freedom for "the best use of a person" through two structural changes: a new work relationship and social units larger than the nuclear family. Maslow (1971) had written about eupsychian, that is, utopian, management in organization, and communal life has been tried, especially in Israel, recently. McWhinney's design for the evolution of social institutions was directly planned for the interaction of individuals, work, and community as a means of personal development—the expansion of the ego through community membership.

G. In Los Angeles this year an AHP-sponsored conference took place which had as its theme "Strategies for Human Liberation." "Liberation" here meant that of children, the aged, men, women, and minorities. It was a term applied to the opening up of organizations and political, educational, family, work, and health institutions. This enormous range of applicability shows the width and depth of the relevance of these social issues in contemporary lives. What is new here, for humanistic psychology, is widespread recognition of the effects of membership in culture and class on the development of persons. Even newer is the search for responsible and effective means of affecting the social ambient to make positive human potentialities become actual. This is not a religious task but a secular one, for the environment is to be utilized, not transcended. It is seen as an opportunity, not as a guaranteed resource.

H. Whereas the current president, Vin Rosenthal, pointed out rightly that the Association for Humanistic Psychology has not been a social-action group, he went on to suggest that the group also cannot "stand as a power for truth in the world" (1976, p. 6). I disagree with this statement. Broad truths are evolutionary; simple ones come and go. If psychologists do not offer access to contemporary truths, what can they offer? Rosenthal also expressed the belief that fulfilling oneself as an individual would automatically require one's concern for the environment and the "co-wellbeing of my fellow persons" (p. 6). Until recently, humanistic psychology has not, however, been concerned with the social determinants of self-actualization.

Although Rosenthal sees a focus on "humanizing and changing existing instituions," he believes that it "is in the area of social action and institutional change . . . that we do not have a strongly mandated mission" (p. 6). It is true that psychology has not had that mandate in the past, but today it is growing.

I. Two pages later, in the same AHP news report, Jack Marvin (1976) suggested an evolutionary step for humanistic psychology: the development of systems or structure that would provide the specialized knowledge of the field (and that of other helping professions) to the solution of social problems. This could be done through a problem-focused review board, using a catalog of demonstrated expertise from which to draw a taskforce that would be dissolved when no longer needed. Marvin remarks that he has been told that AHP is strictly an interest group and that action is left to other organizations. However, he believes that movement toward action is inevitable. Others agree. We can choose to act or not to do so; we can choose among the possible actions to decide which we will take. Future reality is dependent on our choices—together, as well as alone—for our beings are, and will continue to be, shaped by the choices of other individuals, as well as of ourselves.

Is this to suggest, as Peter Marin (1975) has, that "a collective creation and habituation of value sustains . . . the 'individual self'"? That private pleasure or self-actualization is impossible in its richest form without communion and community? Marin wrote in criticism that, in humanistic psychology, "The self replaces community, relation, neighbor, chance, or God . . . The web of reciprocity and relation is broken. The felt presence of the other disappears, and with it a part of our own existence" (p. 48). But beyond the self lie the "worlds of community and value, the worlds of history and action . . . to be entered as a moral man or woman among other persons, with a person's real and complex nature and needs" (p. 50).

Marin would abandon the self or at least diminish its centrality for the sake of community and reciprocity among persons. His criticism is moving, but is it valid? What he does not see is that what he calls narcissism is not, in any case, all there is to humanistic psychology. It was not so in the past, and there are clear signs that it will not be so in the future.

We have the freedom to act individually, but that does not free us from recognizing the real character of human association. For each individual, each self, there is a transindividual situation involved. Personal acts, based on relationships between social values and individual consciousness, are constituent elements in the development or change of social units, just as social units which are meaningful composites shape the person. Self-knowledge is a basis for social action in democratic societies (and a therapist may be an effective change agent). But self-definition is a result, in large part, of social definition. The ideological shape of the society, in its complex manifestations, maims or heals the individual.

How the individual develops is contingent upon the context in which development occurs. Dehumanization is the result of damaging social structures and processes where the person is not free of function as a person. Full and positive existence depends on the nurturance provided within the social system. Martin Buber (1965) expressed this well when he wrote that the "inmost growth of the self is not accomplished . . . in relation to himself, but in the relation between the one and the other . . . one is made present in his own self by the other" (p. 116). The large question is what can institutions, groups, all aspects of the social system be to provide opportunities for optimal growth for all, regardless of social class, sex, and age. The description of ideal life is not enough, however intuitive, metaphoric, and beautiful. Amelioration requires action.[6]

THE FUTURE

Where does the future lie? Not in allegiance to specific techniques, but in the enlargement of methodologies that integrate self-knowledge with knowledge of the larger world—the perception of reality extended outwardly as well as inwardly. This would include the search for positive self-knowledge within the formal curriculum of the schools, all of them. Education should be the widening and deepening of consciousness, bearing in mind that reality must be directly experienced.

When Bugental (1967) collected the opinions of his co-authors, he asked them to describe what they believed to be the future direction of humanistic psychology. Responses included creative and healthy changes in human experience, increased openness and freedom, as much attention to inner life as to behavior, genuine communication in an authentic community, the unfolding of vast capabilities and latent human capacities, the therapist as existential guide disclosing his own state of being, the study of the good and the beautiful (using values and feelings as data) as well as what is true, a chemical breakthrough to creativity and the possibility for human response using extrasensory perception, and the exploration of the supraconscious, that is, the creative unconscious.

This was an impressive and inspiring list, but its omission was dramatic: only one author saw humanistic psychology put to work in social planning and governmental practices, as well as in individual change. Personal fulfillment was simply not seen as a political or social issue to the degree to which it is today. In the past humanistic psychology has been utilized in education, research, industrial management, race relations, community organization, and family relations, as well as psychotherapy (Richards & Welch, 1973). Its future will be even more comprehensive. It will include a deepending and accelerated emphasis on the application of humanistic insights to social issues.

What is the *human* nature of human nature? Clearly, it is an expanding ideal that is yet to be achieved, a description of an aspiration and a hope for future accomplishment. Sisyphus rolled his rock endlessly toward the heights, only to have it crash below over and over again. Yet, like Albert Camus (1955), we must imagine that he was happy, as long as he believed that his task could be accomplished. Human nature is a phenomenon of belief that is still developing and unfolding. It is a phenomenon with enduring social consequences, for everything we choose to do is based on certain concepts of the nature of humanness.

What is known about the power of the social-psychological determinants of human behavior compels the conclusion that . . . men and women must believe that mankind can become fully human in order for our species to attain its humanity . . . a soberly optimisic view of man's potential . . . is a precondition for social action to make actual that which is possible. (Eisenberg, 1972, p. 124)

We are, in short, the active mediators of our own existence. Shall we, then, accept *Ulysses'* invitation as Alfred, Lord Tennyson, wrote it?

I cannot rest from travel . . .
I am a part of all that I have met;
Yet all experience is an arch where
    through gleams that untraveled world
    whose margin fades forever and
    forever when I move . . .
This gray spirit yearns in desire to
    follow knowledge like a sinking star,
Beyond the utmost bounds of human thought . . .
The lights begin to twinkle from the rocks,
The long day wanes: the slow moon climbs:
The deep moans round with many voices.
Come my friends,
'Tis not too late to seek a newer world.

References

Allport, G. W. *Becoming: Basic considerations for a philosophy of personality.* New Haven, Con.: Yale University Press, 1955.

Brain, L. *Science and man.* New York: American Elsevier, 1966.

Buber, M. *Between man and man.* New York: Macmillan, 1965.

Bugental, J. F. T. The humanistic ethic: The individual in psychotherapy as a societal change agent. *Journal of Humanistic Psychology,* 1971, *11,* 11—25.

Bugental, J. F. T. (Ed.). *Challenges of humanistic psychology.* New York: McGraw-Hill, 1967.

Bugental, J. F. T. *The search for authenticity: An existential-analytic approach to psychotherapy.* New York: Holt, Rinehart and Winston, 1965.

Bugental, J. F. T. Humanistic psychology: A new breakthrough. *American Psychologist,* 1963, *18,* 563—567.

Buhler, C., & Allen, M. *Introduction to humanistic psychology.* Monterey, Ca.: Brooks/Cole, 1972.

Buhler, C., & Massarik, F. *The course of human life: A study of goals in the humanistic perspective.* New York: Springer, 1968.

Camus, A. *The myth of Sisyphus and other essays.* New York: Knopf, 1955.

Combs, A. W., & Snygg, D. *Individual behavior: A perceptual approach to behavior.* (Revised Ed.), New York: Harper & Row, 1959.

Eisenberg, L. The human nature of human nature. *Science,* 1972, *176,* 123–128.

Fantini, M. *The people and their school: Community participation.* Bloomington, Ind.: Phi Delta Kappan, 1975.

Gale, R. F. *Developmental behavior: A humanistic approach.* New York: Macmillan, 1969.

Giorgi, A. *Psychology as a human science: A phenomenologically based approach.* New York: Harper & Row, 1970.

Goldstein, K. *The organism: A holistic approach to biology derived from pathological data in man.* New York: American Book, 1939.

Hoover, E. New psychology: New image of man. *Los Angeles Times,* 1975. (Reprinted in *AHP Newsletter,* August 1975, pp. 11–13).

Jourard, S., Growing awareness and the awareness of growth. In H. Otto, J. Mann (Eds.), *Ways of growth.* New York: Grossman, 1965.

Krippner, S. Presidential Address, Association for Humanistic Psychology, 1974.

Landsman, T. One's best self. In S. Jourard (Ed.), *To be or not to be: Existential-psychological studies of the self.* University of Florida Social Science Monographs, 1967, No. 34, 37–50.

Mann, J. H. *Frontiers of psychology.* New York: Macmillan, 1963.

Marin, P. The new narcissism. *Harper's Magazine,* October 1975, pp. 45–56.

Marvin, J. From interest to action: An evolutionary step for AHP. *AHP Newsletter,* June 1976, p. 8.

Maslow, A. H. *The farther reaches of human nature.* New York: Harper, 1971.

Maslow, A. H. *Motivation and personality* (1st ed.). New York: Harper, 1954.

Maslow, A. H. A philosophy of psychology: The need for a mature science of human nature. In F. T. Severin (Ed.), *Humanistic viewpoints in psychology: A book of readings.* New York: McGraw-Hill, 1965.

May, R. *Psychology and the human dilemma.* Princeton, N.J.: Van Nostrand, 1967.

McWhinney, W. Phenomenarchy: A suggestion for social redesign. *Journal of Applied Behavior,* 1973, *9,* 163–180.

Richards, R., & Welch, I. D. *Sightings: Essays in humanistic psychology.* Boulder, Colo.: Shields Publishing, 1973.

Rogers, C. The place of the person in the new world of the behavioral sciences. *Personnel and Guidance Journal,* 1955/1956, *34,* 442–451.

Rosenthal, V. Perspectives on the third force and the third front, *AHP Newsletter*, June 1976, p. 6.

Rubin, J. Yesterday's rebel becomes today's Guru. *Los Angeles Times*, June 13, 1976, Part II, p. 5.

Severin, F. T. (Ed.). *Humanistic viewpoints in psychology: A book of readings*. New York: McGraw-Hill, 1965.

Shklar, J. N. Hegel's phenomenology: The moral failures of asocial man. *Political Theory*, 1973, *1*, 259−286.

Sutich, A. Editorial. *Journal of Transpersonal Psychology*, 1969, *1*, iv.

Tart, C. T. (Ed.) *Transpersonal psychologies*. New York: Harper & Row, 1975.

Teilhard de Chardin, P. *The phenomenon of man* (Rev. ed.). New York: Harper & Row, 1965.

Tillich, P. *The courage to be*. New Haven, Conn.: Yale University Press, 1952.

Watson, R. I. Psychology: A prescriptive science. *American Psychologist*, 1967, *22*, 435−443.

Welch, I. D. Position: Humanistic or missionary? *AHP Newsletter*, October, 1975, p. 11.

Footnotes

[1] Within humanistic psychology, the definition of humanness tends to be relatively homogeneous. See, for example, May (1967) who describes human beings as mammal; as animals who talk and use symbols as language; who keep time, past, present, and future, and have a time-binding capacity even beyond death; who have awareness of history and the capacity for social interaction, as well as the capacity for the transcendence of concrete situations and abstractions. Human beings are also bound up with self-relatedness and consciously, intellectually self-aware they are deeply involved with the weighing of consequences and the development of ethical systems. (p. 193)

[2] See, for example, Mann (1963). Although including parapsychology in the frontiers described (along with space travel, computers, teaching machines, communications theory, and creativity and intelligence), Mann suggested that one tenth of 1% of psychologists were ac-

tively interested in it and that his discussion was going "against the tide of current psychological thought and belief" (p. 168). As soon as 5 years later, together with Otto, he described avenues of self-exploration that have been basic to any delineation of humanistic psychology: play, breathing therapy, sensory awakening, encounter, peak-experiences, Gestalt, the creative subself, dreams, meditation, the psychedelic experience, and transcendent functioning, that is, the full use of potentialities (Otto & Mann, 1968).

[3] The list of composite factors of the best self varies from widened and deepened consciousness to this typical description by Ted Landsman (1967) which includes: "IQ, productivity, actualized talent, sensitivity, warmth, skill in human relationships, courage, kindness, gentleness and capacity to help in conflict resolution or to help in general." Each list will vary.

[4] Originally this association was the American Association for Humanistic Psychology. Dropping the national designation was a clear reach toward its worldwide constituency.

[5] Anthony Sutich, in the first issue of the *Journal of Transpersonal Psychology* in the spring of 1969, referred to transpersonal, or spiritual, psychology as the "Fourth Force." He defined it as the

> *empirical*, scientific study of, and responsible implementation of the finds relevant to becoming, individual and species-wide meta-needs, ultimate values, unitive consciousness, peak experiences, B-values, ecstasy, mystical experience, awe, being, self-actualization, essence, bliss, wonder, ultimate meaning, transcendence of the self, spirit, oneness, cosmic awareness, individual and species-wide synergy, maximal interpersonal encounter, sacralization of everyday life, transcendal phenomena, cosmic self-humor and playfulness, maximal sensory awareness, responsiveness and expression, and related concepts, experiences and activities . . . (p. iv).

This complicated list is elaborated and explained in Charles Tart's (1975) book on the transpersonal psychologies in which he attempts to integrate the spiritual and the scientific to develop state-specific sciences that draw from both scientific tradition and human, spiritual potentialities. This work includes a fine analysis of the assumptions of scientific, Western psychology and compares them to transpersonal theory, making a contrast between the physicalistic world and the *para*(that is, "beyond") normal phenomena of ESP and other kinds of perception and action.

[6] For this reason it seems to be no accident that humanistic psychology developed so fully in this country. In few places in the world could it have grown so rapidly to this extent. The relative freedom of the social environment, as well as a broad economic middle class, made it possible.

5

Human Priorities

EDWIN N. BARKER

*W*hen I began this chapter, I knew that I wanted to discuss some possible futures of human beings on this planet as a base for a consideration of desirable "new frontiers" to be explored by psychologists. Several titles came to mind. "Frontiers in Humanistic Psychology" was one possibility. Another was, "If the World Appears to Be Just About Doomed, How Might it Possibly *Not* be?" "How Might the World Be Saved?" also came to mind. "What To Do Until the Savior Comes" was rejected as too flippant, in favor of the more restrained "Human Priorities."

OUR LIKELY FUTURE

First—a picture of where I think we are now, as a foundation for some speculations about the future and the choices about priorities we must make. What do the people say whose life work is the systematic study of possible futures? When I look at what futurologists, economists, computer model people, food experts, ecologists, population and political analysts, say, I have to admit that their evidence is impressive—doubly impressive because many of them, independently, have come up with almost identical predictions. If you accept the method of discerning current trends and extrapolating likely futures, I think you would have to conclude that it is possibly just about over for civilization as we know it on this planet! Even more striking is that methods other than straight extrapolations of current trends predict the same future. Equations that take into account some really major ameliorative changes and possible corrective actions (such as an immediate crash program to change what we are doing to the ecology or to diminish population growth) still predict a disastrous future.

What are some of the issues that the "future experts" consider? Political analysts dwell on the bomb. Considering the accelerating dissemination of nuclear power technology to more and more countries (who are not any less sane than the super powers, but who could believe they have less to lose by unleashing such force) these analysts conclude that there is a moderate to high probability that thriving human life will not be on this planet in 50 years. That is, we are going to blow it up, unless some intervention occurs that we do not now foresee. The evidence seems clear that there is no significant progress in arms control, certainly no slow down. On the contrary, we face an acceleration in both the dissemination of the knowledge of how to build nuclear weapons and in the deployment of them.

But let us say we avoid blowing ourselves up. Even then many analysts agree that, unless trends somehow change, somewhere between 20 to 50 years from now there will be a precipitous, a catastrophic, decline in the quality of life on the whole planet. It may be more dramatic in so-called developed countries because we have more to lose. But, we all face a crisis, developed and underdeveloped countries alike. We will no longer have clean air and clean water. There will be a drastic plummeting of living standards. Futurologists come to this conclusion by examining, among other things, the rate at which we are polluting our environment; the rate of depletion of our resources for energy, for building, for food; and the fact that over one-half of the population of this earth is now hungry most of the time.

But the situation is even worse than the futurologists predict with their rational analysis of current trends. These analysts are hard heads, they look at hard data, and they do not bring into their equations another element that greatly complicates the problem: the obscene maldistribution of power and wealth and justice on this planet, which increases tensions within and between people and decreases the possibility of even a civil atmosphere between human beings. A clear distinction exists between the upper-third as compared to the southern two-thirds of the globe, which is largely a white/nonwhite distinction. The old adage, "the rich get richer and the poor get poorer," instead of becoming less true, in the last few decades has become *more* true.

The projections converge. The world is going downhill fast. If that is indeed true, then the world or life at least as humane as we have known it, can only be saved by an unprecedentedly rapid, an unprecedentedly radical and major transformation in human action—only if human beings in sufficient numbers and with sufficient influence become in some sense "more enlightened" than we have any hope now to believe they will.

HOW TO CHANGE THE FUTURE?

I know of only two scenarios (or two meanings of that phrase, "more enlightened") that might reasonably be expected to alter that future: (1) if human beings get "smarter" or (2) if human beings get "nicer." I first consider the possibilities of "getting smarter."

A Scenario Based on Hubris

Radical changes could occur if human beings in large numbers became cognitively smarter, had more enlightened self-interest, could see much more clearly the consequences of their actions: those consequences that are distal as well as proximal in time, those long-term as well as short-term effects, those indirect as well as direct outcomes—the consequences of our actions in relation to each other and in relation to our planet. *Maybe*, if we got amazingly smarter, amazingly quickly, we could alter our future. But, I believe this is the strategy human beings *have been* attempting. It has been tried, and tried, and tried. At least since the rationalist enlightenment the thrust has been toward intellectual-instrumental-technocratic solutions: attempts toward a rational world government, toward true democracies, toward efficient and beneficial technocracies of greater and greater complexity, toward the planned state idea of providing social justice and equal goods for all. We have tried to be *smart* enough to solve our problems, to use our intellect to find a way to live harmoniously together on this planet. We have devised "management by objectives" to try to make things work, and we have "planning-programming-budgeting systems" to allocate resources in the most rational way possible to serve the most people.

My understanding of history and my understanding of the nature of persons lead me to conclude that reliance on the strategy of succeeding solely by being smarter has failed, is failing, and will continue to fail. That approach has not stopped the production of bombs, has not slowed down pollution or started resource saving programs, has not reduced the population explosion. People have not accepted the evidence that until the dispossessed on this planet are on a par with the rest of us, there is no possibility for a civil environment, no hope for a thriving economy, no chance of world peace. A chilling critique of the fallacy of relying on intelligence alone to solve problems is outlined by Halberstam (1972) in his book *The Best and the Brightest*. He indicts the reference group that I, and most of you reading this, belong to: affluent, liberal, white, upper-middle class, educated, conditioned to have faith in technocracy and its solutions. His analysis is devastating.

If it is true then that the strategy of trying to be more rational *only*, brighter *only*, has not worked—why hasn't it? I see two possible reasons why it has not worked and why it will continue not to work as a sole approach.

One reason it has not worked may be that human beings have developed social and technological systems of such complexity that at this point in evolution we simply *cannot* be smart enough to control them. We have outdone ourselves. We have created entities that we cannot control, and with such interlocking complexity that we certainly cannot see clearly the long-term and indirect effects of our actions. It may be that human beings do not know enough because we *cannot* know enough. Maybe our species simply does not have the brain power yet to handle, for example, an organization of 7 million people such as exists in New York City. It may simply be too complex for our heads to handle.

If our intellect has created organizations too complex to understand and if we cannot control all this technology, one solution could be as Gandhi (Fischer, 1962) tried to sell to India, to lead a simpler life by eschewing much of modern technocracy. Gandhi hoped that India would go the route of cottage industry for quite a few generations and not follow the modern nation path of capital development and impersonal mass government. His wisdom went unheeded in his own country and it does not seem likely now that we are willing to forego this thing we have valued so much: our complex technology with its material results *and* with its inevitable supporting technocratic values.

Another reason why "getting smarter" has not worked: at times it seems as though we *do* know enough. Sometimes it appears as though we do have solutions to our complex problems. But human beings do not implement the solutions. We do not pay attention. Emotionally, people do not accept solutions that require drastic, or even inconvenient, changes. We distort and deny for present comfort. For example, some years back the Kerner Commission (National Advisory Commission, 1968) analyzed the situation in this country regarding racism, poverty, and violence. They did an analysis of some causes and effects and possible solutions and concluded that the continuation of current trends would lead to increasing strife or malaise. Their reports have hardly had an impact!

However, it is not only complex problems we fail to face, but simpler ones as well. For quite a while now it has been very clear to anybody who has studied it that the automobile is killing us. We simply *cannot* in this country, with the population concentration that we have, rely on highways and automobiles as we currently do. It is no longer possible for a person to say, "I can drive my car anywhere and whenever I like." We are killing our cities and we are killing ourselves. We have known this for a long time, but we have not even *begun* to change from the individual automobile to mass transportation.

Even if we intellectually can determine the solution to some of our complex problems, deeply held attitudes often trip us up. Clearly, in our current environments, human beings are often not motivated by rationality, long-term self-interest, *or* by informed caring and empathy for our species or our planet.

A Scenario Based on Wish-fulfillment

So, how about the second way that might avert our predicted sad future: human beings could get "nicer?" The scenario might be different if somehow or other large numbers of people became at a gut level, in a *felt* sense, more emotionally loving and caring of themselves and others, more immediately empathic to self and others and things: if human beings objectified less, anthropomorphized more, accepted the universal nature of themselves and their connection and mutual dependency with all people and all things; if they felt, *experienced*, the relationship between themselves and all things. That is pretty dramatic. That might save us. We know very little about changes like that, radical changes in consciousness, deep value changes. Historically, we have called those kinds of changes, "the birth of new religions." Those kinds of changes rarely happen and appear to have followed the appearance of a charismatic, or "divine," if you like, leader, or teacher.

But we surely can do more than hope for a new messiah. The apocalyptic nature of our predicted future will not change unless we ourselves change. Getting smarter will not do it alone, and we cannot *will* ourselves and others to be "nicer," wiser, more open, more caring.

SO, WHAT DO WE DO?

The only thing that makes any sense as far as I can see is for humanistic psychologists, for humans in general, to consider very carefully that "niceness" dimension—those intangibles like empathy, caring, authenticity and openness, experientially construing human beings in terms based on human experience rather than on abstractions or nonhuman mechanical objects.

Apparently, human beings do not get the gut feelings of caring, empathy, openness, respect, or love of self, others, or nature by rational argument. It has been tried and tried. And we know very little about the conditions that *are* conducive to such proactive and prosocial processes. As Bevan (1976) says, "We must now look . . . in the unexplored regions of the human mind and in the poorly understood principles that govern the function of human institutions" (p. 485). Bevan argues that, "the reason for our predicament and our only hope for survival are one and the same: 'the human capacity to discover and apply new knowledge'" (p. 484). I would argue that the reason for our predicament is an overreliance on *a particular mode* of discovering and applying new knowledge, and that our only hope for survival lies in learning a new way to learn! And soon.

A NEW MEANING OF "GETTING SMARTER"

Past attempts at political and social change, as well as past attempts at psychological research, have been similar in their characteristics: a deliberate distancing of the "subjects" by the planners/researchers, a concern with efficient control and manipulation, an obsession with easily observed external results or easy quantifications, a lack of intimate knowledge of the experiential inner-worlds or felt-needs of the "target population," an absence of "participant-democracy" or collaboration between "subjects" and "researchers." Past efforts have been characterized by what David Bakan (1966) would call "unmitigated agency . . . The villain is unmitigated agency. The moral imperative is to try to mitigate agency with communion" (p. 14).

I am arguing, along with Rae Carlson (1972), that, "Agentic (masculine) modes of inquiry involving manipulation, quantification, and, control need to be complemented by the communal (feminine) research styles (naturalistic, qualitative, open) . . ." (pg. 17). Why? For one thing because we discover very different "facts" when we ask the detached observers (agentic researchers/planners) than when we ask the actors/subjects (Jones, 1976). Let me be clear. I am not only saying that we must use our "smartness" to study different topics (the "humanistic" ones). I am saying that we must be smart (investigate) in new ways, regardless of the topic. And, I postulate that learning to understand (investigate, "be smart") in certain ways will lead to more humane ways of "taking action" (improving, healing, reforming, "making revolution").

What will these new ways of studying persons look like? We know very little about that at this point, but the issue is beginning to be addressed (e.g., Barker, 1971/72; Giorgi, 1970; Rosini, 1976; Shlien, 1970). That it can be done is clear. Using research methods which took seriously people's reports of their experiencing, Larry Rosini (1976) studied the experience of being dehumanized by being treated as an object. He concluded,

> . . . the method is useful. It took on a phenomenon that had been impressionistically described and variously discussed in a number of contexts; but in ways that allowed for no clear-cut definition of the phenomenon, especially in its psychological dimensions. The method enabled the discovery that the experience does have boundaries, and within them a distinct pattern. The experience of dehumanization, which seemed at the start to have an inexhaustible number of manifestations, turned out to be a limited field, with internal regularity and discernible elements. It is not a phenomenon that is chaotic, or one that has only idiosyncratic expressions. It is identifiable—measurable, in a true sense—on a finite terrain, with discernible if mutually interactive differentiations. As a result, the way is paved for further inquiries that stem from it (p. 153).

We are not without models for attempts at an integration of new ways of being "smart" and "nice," people who have used our current knowledge in attempting to become as fully human as possible, who have created environments conducive to being open to themselves and others, and who have rigorously used their intellect and rationality to further their understanding of that non-rational, gut-level stuff. Sidney Jourard combined those two, trying systematically to find the order in the data of nature but always in the context of listening to the concrete human being. His colleague, Ted Landsman, is another who has been willing to take on the task of studying the "soft" subjects without sacrificing rigor and tough-mindedness. The work of Gendlin (1962) exemplifies what I am talking about, as does the study done by Shulman (1976) which furthered our understanding of what "helping" means by paying attention to the subjective experience of people concerning "helpful others" in everyday life. The work reported by Epting et al. in this volume indicates both the difficulty of our task as well as the exciting implications of the interlocking nature of the results when one studies such seemingly disparate topics as authenticity, person-perception, and therapeutic conditions.

Two people of my time have been most influential in shaping the model I have in mind. One is Carl Rogers, who has critically examined the human condition without disengaging from it. He has been an evidence-seeking research scientist in the best meaning of the term while remaining deeply involved and nonmanipulative with persons and a logical and rational architect of significant theory without reverting to terms and analogies alien to human experience. Outside our own field, another model for me is Martin Luther King, Jr. He followed a carefully articulated strategy for social change and was possibly the toughest, most sophisticated political operator of our time. But his tactics manifested a philosophy of, and experiencing of, all human beings as inherently worthy of authentic respect, mutuality, and empathic caring. Using your head and using your heart are not incompatible.

CAUTIONARY REMARKS

If we are to contribute to the evolution of a model of the human person that is based on human experience (and I believe that is the only way our world will survive), we must become increasingly hardheaded while simultaneously becoming increasingly softhearted. We must neither desert our involvement with the subtle and complex phenomena as experienced by real, sensate people day to day, nor reject demands for evidence and logic, nor the tools of science and scholarship. We must speak convincingly to the standards of scientists and scholars—but not only to them. We must become skilled in "giving away" our results (and our evidence) and our methods directly to the public. This, of course, should always be the attempt of all science, but it is especially true now (because time may be running out) and it is especially true for us (because our goal is to create a science that is not esoteric, but in terms drawn from human experience).

There now exist a few centers where serious humanistic science is being attempted (e.g., Duquesne University and the Humanistic Psychology Institute). We must be aware that such attempts will face strong pressures *not* to produce humanistic searchers but to revert to the usual technocratic-engineering model. The economics of the job market, the intellectual defensiveness engendered by being in the "third force" instead of "the main stream," the sheer conceptual magnitude of our task—all make it tempting to go back either to conventional, manipulative, trivial, "objective" psychological research or to "intuitive," dramatic, packaged, pretending of skills in social or personal "intervention" without a theoretical or evidential foundation.

Although the human potential movement initially appeared to offer a welcome corrective to some of the authoritarian tendencies in psychiatry, psychoanalysis, and behaviorism, there are evidences that it, too, is succumbing to the technocratic-engineering mode. Through "hot seats," group pressure sessions, directives from gurus, "exercises," "fish bowls," "designed workshops," the message (though couched in humanistic words) seems to be, "*We* know what health is, and we will intervene to make you better." That is *not* what I would call the desirable new frontier of humanistic psychology.

There are clear signs, also, of the human potential movement succumbing to what I would call the old, familiar "capitalistic-huckster" mode: The "I've got the latest, new, improved therapy (or social change) technique. And I have a new Association, Institute, Journal, and letterhead to prove it!" And all this without a shred of evidence, exactly analogous to misleading advertising in business.

With our technocratic conditioning, it is *so* difficult to retain the stance of learners and searchers, without wanting to become (or have the appearance of being) human/social engineers. And yet, it is my conclusion that attaining that stance of the learner is *the* task of our time.

The body of research of Carl Rogers and his colleagues (Hart & Tomlinson, 1970), and, for example, of Giorgi (1970), Shulman (1976), Rosini (1976), and Gordon (1976) lead me to the tremendously exciting hypothesis that really "being smart" and "being nice" are much the same thing. That is, there may be a common characteristic of the best pure scientist (of persons), the best therapist, the best social change agent, and the most ethical person. In all cases, the key characteristic may be *a noninterfering interest in empathically understanding the phenomenon in its own terms*, without bias (as is so often true in "therapy" and social change efforts) and without distancing "objectification" (as in traditional science). It may be that the most effective pure scientist of persons and the most helpful change agent are more like each other than either is like an engineer.

IN A NUTSHELL . . .

Planning and intervention based on impersonal observation and detached rationality are best suited to accomodate machinery—hard, compact material. But for soft little animals like we human beings, who are a strange mix of tough and tender, easy to bruise and harden over, somewhat contrary and unpredictable animals—planning with us or helping us to live together on this planet require a mix of realism and empathy, agency and communion, rationality and compassionate intuition, accurate knowledge of our proper care and feeding, plus the capacity to be touched by our imperfections.

Experiencing respect for the intrinsic worth of others *as they are* has been thought of as "only" a religious attitude. And yet, it is fast becoming clear that there is no chance for a civil social environment, an adequate economic order, an orderly succession of power, even, possibly, our physical survival, without a change toward valuing all human beings as ends in themselves and not as means to other ends. This has not been felt to be a political, utilitarian, instrumental, practical attitude, and *certainly* not a "scientific," "realistic," one. Our task is to change that.

References

Bakan, D. *The duality of human existence.* Chicago: Rand-McNally, 1966.

Barker, E. N. Humanistic psychology and scientific method. *Interpersonal Development,* 1971/72, *2,* 137–172.

Bevan, W. The sound of the wind that's blowing. *American Psychologist,* 1976, *31,* 481–491.

Carlson, R. Understanding women: Implications for personality theory and research. *Journal of Social Issues,* 1972, *28,* 17–32.

Fischer, L. (Ed.). *The essential Gandhi.* New York: Vintage, 1962.

Gendlin, E. *Experiencing and the creation of meaning: A philosophical and psychological approach to the subjective.* New York: Free Press, 1962.

Giorgi, A. Phenomenology and experiential research: I. In A. Giorgi, W. F. Fisher, & R. von Eckartsberg (Eds.), *Duquesne studies in phenomenological psychology* (Vol. 1). Pittsburgh: Duquesne University Press, 1970.

Gordon, B. *The experience of being treated as "mentally ill."* Unpublished doctoral dissertation, Harvard University, 1976.

Halberstam, D. *The best and the brightest.* New York: Random House, 1972.

Hart, J. T., & Tomlinson, T. M. (Eds.). *New directions in client-centered therapy.* Boston: Houghton Mifflin, 1970.

Jones, E. E. How do people perceive the causes of behavior? *American Scientist,* 1976, *64,* 300–305.

National Advisory Commission on Civil Disorders. *Report of the National Advisory Commission on Civil Disorders.* New York: Dutton, 1968.

Rosini, L. A. *Being treated as a subject: The structure of the experience of dehumanization.* Unpublished doctoral dissertation, Harvard University, 1976.

Shlien, J. M. Phenomenology and personality. In J. T. Hart & T. M. Tomlinson (Eds.), *New directions in client-centered therapy.* Boston: Houghton Mifflin, 1970.

Shulman, D. G. *Correlates of being perceived as helpful in informal interpersonal relationships.* Unpublished doctoral dissertation, Harvard University, 1976.

6

Feminism and Humanism

DOROTHY D. NEVILL

Social movements and social change have as their impetus a sense of dissatisfaction with the current situation, whatever condition exists at the moment. The left out, the disadvantaged, the passed-over, the disenfranchised, if left in that condition long enough, begin to want to move, to grow, to expand, to claim for themselves that part of the world that has been denied to them. Such changes can occur through orderly evolution or through violent revolution. The force of the method is dependent in some degree on the amount of festering frustration that has accumulated over time.

Violent revolution results in the blood baths of the French Revolution and the riots of Watts. Orderly evolution results in gradual, peaceful change of the social system spurred on by the efforts of those involved. Regardless of the nature of the protest, any social movement must contain the whole gamut of political activity in order to accomplish its purpose. Those who press for change must be united philosophically, but be diverse in tactic.

There must be the active force, radical if you will, pressing publicly with at least some hint of violence, for immediate change. There must be the active, though establishment-oriented, element working with the existing culture to consolidate and implement the changes that are desired. In between must be all shades of active, dedicated members. Without the efforts of the "street brigades" the work of the more conservative appears weak and ineffectual. Without the efforts of the "bridge builders" the violent often splinter from society and have only themselves to listen to, or if powerful enough, lunge and lurch, almost accidentally, into war and catastrophe.

We are living through one of the most far-reaching evolutionary periods in our civilization. Women and men have begun to look at long sacrosanct sexual stereotypes and to question their continued necessity. "Why must our potentiality be limited in terms of our sexuality?" "Why cannot the opportunity of experiencing wholeness be extended to each one of us?" "Why are laws allowed which limit and regulate us because we are one sex or another?" "Why do we place value judgements on activities because they are engaged in predominantly by one sex?"

Questions such as these are only possible because of an unprecedented situation. For the first time in our history, the biology of the female reproductive system is clear and can with a high degree of probability be predicted and controlled. Never before in our history has this simple fact been true. Parents can choose whether or not to have children. Children can be born into a world where each one is loved and desired. Compulsory pregnancy can be an incident of the past. Women can enter into the fullness of life with the freedom to choose the manner in which they wish to participate.

Such has not always been true. In the past women have been accorded a more limited, more protected status than men because of biological necessity. Women become pregnant. During this time their bodies are not as lithe and capable as at other times. In an earlier age, without adequate means of refrigeration or pasteurization, the safest food for newborns was mother's milk. Extended lactation increased a woman's dependency. Women were in an almost continual state of bearing or caring for children.

It was not from a vacuum that adages such as "barefoot and pregnant" and "a tooth for every child" arose. The vast majority of women, with only a few exceptions of the unusually wealthy or talented, agreed to accept a lesser role in the non-life-productive world, what we have called "man's world." With the establishment of a different status for women it was inevitable that abuses crept into the system so that women have been, at times, regarded as inferior, incapable, fit only for "women's work."

But now, the situation has changed, the cycle has been broken. Women, like men, can choose, to some extent, their destiny. It is hard to envision the far-reaching implications of this change in our lifestyle. For the first time we are consciously deciding on appropriate sex role patterns. What will be the implications for family constellations, child-rearing patterns, economic dependency, patriarchal religion, and other central part of our lives? Our lives are already undergoing the inevitable changes. If one were to list the 100 most influential people of the past century in the United States, the name of Margaret Sanger would probably not appear on a single list. But this woman, who almost single-handedly brought birth control to this country, who got together the monied individuals and the interested scientists in order to develop the "pill," probably has had as significant an impact on our style of living as any other individual that we could name.

A new social movement has arisen to guide the evolutionary change, one would hope, in a loving fashion: called pejoratively by its detractors as "women's lib," known to its intimates as "feminism." Unfortunately the image conjured up in most people's minds by the term feminism is that engendered by the national media, which publicizes the more radical, activist branch of the movement: the fictitious and legendary, bra-burning, lesbian man-haters. Perhaps women like this do exist. But the movement is far more than the press implies. All women are far more united philosophically than the media assumes. The movement embraces degrees of activism differing along the political spectrum from the Association of University Women to the Redstockings. But, the degree of politicism is not the pertinent dimension . What is important is the philosophy that unites feminists of all persuasions, an underlying feminist philosophy which is akin to the basic tenets of humanism, of self-actualization, of the whole human potential movement.

But, I am getting ahead of myself. Let us ask the beginning question first. What is a feminist? We cannot accept popular definitions of feminism, either from a national press attempting to sell their products or from polemic writers who spew hate and division. It is best to go to actual source itself for the data, to the women themselves. What is a feminist?

"a woman who is really aware of womanhood"

"a woman who is aware of her right to everything in life that everyone else has a right to"

"not just a member of a group"

"a woman's claim to happiness and property and money and freedom and independence, all of the things that a person might wish to strive for"

"active, not necessarily an activist"

"a man or a woman or a child that attempts to see people not in relation to their sex but as individuals"

"a broadening of sensitivity, perception, feeling, caring, sharing, all the catchwords of our time, to include everybody"

"recognized in our society as equals"

"growing, loving, caring"

"becoming the best that one can"

"utilizing one's talents to the fullest, regardless of sex"

"being able to choose from the whole gamut of human emotions and experiences, not being arbitrarily limited to only half of life, just because one is female or male."

The theme that is repeated over and over again in these definitions is that of growth, of self-fulfillment, of becoming a truly complete person. The emphasis is on the positive expansion of the individual. It is my contention that the kind of person a feminist desires to become is analogous to that described by Landsman as "beautiful and noble" or by Rogers as "fully functioning" or by Maslow as "self-actualized."

How can this be? How can the focal point of the feminist movement and humanistic psychology be the same? To answer this question we need to carefully look at the implications of sex stereotyping.

A characteristic common to all cultures is the division of tasks according to sex. The extent and rigidity of the assigning varies widely. In some instances it is determined primarily by biological characteristics. Women are expected to bear children and men to perform a greater share of the tasks involving muscular strength. In other instances the workload pertains to far more than that dictated by physical differences and permeates every aspect of living. Either sex might be required to eat only certain foods, to dress differently, or to engage in specific occupations. For example, men might sow a crop, while women tend and harvest it. Not only can the extent of task assignment vary, but also the rigidity with which it must be followed. The reaction to violation of sex role mores in a society can include severe punishment, ostracism, reprimand, condescension, amused tolerance, or relative indifference. Generally societies in which sex stereotyping permeates many areas of life tend to expect rigid adherence to those standards. Those societies that allocate fewer tasks based on sex tend to allow somewhat more flexibility in behavior. There are no societies to my knowledge that assign tasks based only on genital differences.

Occurring alongside the assignment of tasks by sex is the expectation of certain behaviors by females and males. It is as if the whole continuum of human responses has been divided up and allocated partially to each sex. The commonly held stereotype of femininity in our culture includes the following characteristics: talkative, tactful, gentle, religious, neat, quiet, dependent, illogical, and emotional. Men, in contrast, are expected to be aggressive, independent, objective, dominant, active, logical, adventurous, ambitious, and self-confident. There is much in the literature to suggest a general consensus as to the stereotypes and appropriate behavior for each sex. Groups as diverse as clinical psychologists and undergraduate students, when asked to describe socially competent men or women, agree on the divergent characteristics of each sex (Broverman, Broverman, Clarkson, Rosenkrantz, & Vogel, 1970).

Now you and I know that these stereotypes do not hold fast in everyday life. We all know plenty of talkative men or ambitious women. There is far more overlap in acceptable behavior by the two sexes than the stereotype literature would have us believe. In most instances greater within-sex differences are found than between-sex differences.

Why, then, has research in the past emphasized the presence of clearly delineated and relatively rigid categories? The answer lies in our reliance on traditional research methods both in conceptualization and in methodology. In general, psychological research has assumed an "either-or" philosophy, that is, either one is dependent or independent, passive or aggressive, logical or illogical, and so forth. Only rarely is the whole continuum of the human personality taken into consideration. In short, we have tended to look at a multidimensional world through bipolar glasses. This limited and rigid view of the human personality was partly the result of inadequate statistical techniques and partly the result of petty thinking. The effects of this philosophy have been far ranging, but we are talking now specifically about sex stereotyping. Here we have a ready-made bipolar situation: female and male. Experiments have been designed to highlight the differences between the sexes, rather than to focus on the individual. Undergraduate students have been given forced-choice questions ("Is basket-weaving more feminine or masculine?"); have been asked to list behaviors, attitudes, and personality characteristics that they felt differentiated between men and women; and have been required to define their ideal woman or man. The result has been two sets of characteristics that comprise the definitions of femaleness and maleness. If researchers went looking for stereotypes, they were bound to find them. Fortunately, methods and viewpoints change, and the current researcher is obligated to look at familiar situations from a new perspective. Bem (1974), for example, has proposed an alternative to the traditional view of sex stereotyping which has heretofore treated masculinity and femininity as mutually exclusive categories on a bipolar continuum. The Bem sex-role inventory treats femininity and masculinity as independent, unipolar scales, allowing the derivation of a third score, androgeny, which measures the differential endorsement of masculine and feminine traits by the same individual.

What is needed, then, is a fresh look at an old situation. In their own ways both the feminist and the humanistic psychologist are attempting to do this. Both emphasize the expansive growth of the individual toward wholeness, that is, toward encompassing the whole spectrum of human potentialities. For a woman growth might mean uncovering the more aggressive, independent part of her nature. For a man growth might mean discovering tenderness and gentleness in himself in quantities that he had not been able to acknowledge before.

It is the ability to see the complexity of our nature that defines us as fully human: the ability to see ourselves in vastly different lights, as free and slave, as object and subject, as submissive and dominant, as lovable and unlovable. The existence and acknowledgement of such polarities in an individual's life are the source for a rich variety of productivity and fulfillment. However, complexities can lead to tension and conflict. Choices are inevitable, but it is in the complexity and tension that the human consciousness can fully develop. In the past we have tried to avoid this situation by clinging to one pole or another: men to a cluster of traits labeled masculine and women to a cluster of traits labeled feminine. The truly complete individual is one who can courageously live with the tension generated by complexity, who chooses the creativity and fulfillment that is possible there.

Rollo May (1967) distinguishes between two types of anxiety: neurotic and normal. Neurotic anxiety is destructive and constricting. It prevents people from realizing their full potential, from enjoying life to the fullest, from recognizing their own worth. It causes the person to become less human and to become apathetic. Normal anxiety, which results from recognizing and accepting the complexities of life, enables people to accomplish what they want. It mobilized forces and helps meet threatening situations. Instead of being constricting, it is expanding. Instead of desensitizing a person, it enables one to see the real world, to make decisions, and to commit oneself to a way of life.

Anxiety, then, is not to be avoided. It is a necessary and important condition of life. As Kierkegaard has said, "Anxiety is the dizziness of freedom." To dare, to challenge, to live is anxiety-provoking. But not to venture is to lose one's essential humanness; to lose the capacity to act, to relate, to become enraptured; to lose the chance to become complete individuals by embracing all of life with all of its complexities.

The whole person realizes that to live a full life one must

recognize one's total being and with that total being to engage in real encounters, to reach out to other individuals in love and compassion. Such a life involves risks, but it is creatively enriching.

The whole person accepts and relishes the richness of life. That person is not frightened by complexity, but thrives on it. That person values life to the fullest. "Not life, but the good life is to be valued." (Aristotle)

The feminist whether female or male, strives to become this creative, courageous person. The humanistic psychologist holds it as a model for all of us. For different reasons, perhaps, and using different techniques, the twophilosophies grow toward a common goal.

References

Bem, S. L. The measurement of psychological androgyny. *Journal of Consulting and Clinical Psychology*, 1974, 42, 155—162.

Broverman, I. K., Broverman, D. M., Clarkson, F. E., Rosenkrantz, P. S., & Vogel, S. R. Sex-role stereotypes and clinical judgements of mental health. *Journal of Consulting and Clinical Psychology*, 1970, 34, 1—7.

May, R. *Psychology and the human dilemma*. Princeton, N.J.: Van Nostrand, 1967.

III

Frontiers
in Human
Interaction

7

Nancy Mourns

CARL R. ROGERS

While it is fresh in my feelings, I want to write about an incident that occurred in a large workshop. It was a seventeen-day workshop consisting of seventy very diverse people, focused on cognitive and experiential learning. All had been in encounter groups for six sessions in the first six days. There had been special-interest topical groups and almost daily meetings of all seventy people. These community meetings had become deeper and more trusting. This episode occurred on the eighth day in a morning community meeting.

THE EPISODE

(This portion is written in the third person because it is the product of several people. A first draft was prepared, and then it was shown to the major participants, each of whom corrected or rewrote the portion describing his or her own feelings and behavior, to make it conform to the perceived reality. Consequently, I believe it is as accurate a picture as can be obtained. All names are disguised except those of Natalie, my daughter, and my own.)

The group had been discussing, with great sensitivity, listening to all points of view, the issue raised by the fact that some people had brought visitors to the community sessions. Nancy had been one of these, bringing her husband to the previous meeting, but she was not present this morning. A consensus was reached that in the future (without criticizing any person up to this point), anyone thinking of bringing a visitor should first raise the question with the community. The group passed on to another issue.

At this point Nancy arrived, very late. Ralph, trying to be helpful, quickly described to her the conclusion we had reached. None of us gave Nancy opportunity to respond, though evidently she tried. The group went on in its discussion. After a few moments someone sitting close to Nancy called attention to the fact that she was shaking and crying, and the community immediately gave her space for her feelings. At first it seemed that she felt criticized, but Maria gave her a more complete description of what had gone on, and she seemed to accept that she was not being blamed or criticized. But still she was physically trembling, and very upset because she felt she had been cut off. It was not the first time, she said. She had felt cut off before. Encouraged to say more she turned to Natalie, Carl's daughter, and said, "I've felt you as very cold, and you've cut me off twice. I keep calling you Betty (another participant)—I don't know why—and when I came to tell you how sorry I felt about that, you just said that was my problem, and turned away."

Natalie replied that her perception was very different. "I realized you were quite upset because you called me by the wrong name, but I said that though I could see it troubled *you*, it didn't bother me at all. I realize I haven't reached out to you, and I think you do want contact with me, but I don't feel I have rebuffed you."

It seemed that Nancy felt more and more strongly about all this, and that she had not heard, or certainly had not accepted,

Natalie's response. She said that she had observed the close relationship Natalie had with Teresa, a Chicano, and that perhaps it was only with minority persons that Natalie could relate, rather than to her—tall, blonde, and middle class. This led to an angry outburst from Teresa about being stereotyped, and about five minutes was spent in rebuilding the relationship between Nancy and Teresa.

The group brought Nancy back to the issue between herself and Natalie. It seemed obvious that her feelings were so strong that they could not come simply from the incident she mentioned. Joyce said she had noticed that she, Nancy, and Natalie were all similar—tall, slim, blonde—and that perhaps Nancy was feeling that Natalie should at least relate to someone like her, rather than to Teresa who was short and dark. Nancy considered this, wondered if there might be something to it, but clearly was not deeply touched by the idea.

At least two other possible bases for her strong feelings were caringly and tentatively suggested to her. To the first she said, "I'm trying on that hat, but it doesn't seem to fit." To the second she said, "That doesn't seem to fit either."

Carl sat there " . . . feeling completely mystified. I wanted to understand just what it was she was troubled about, but I couldn't get *any* clue to follow. I believe many others were feeling the same way. Here she was with tears in her eyes, feeling something far beyond some possible imaginary rebuff, but what *was* it.?"

Then Ann said, "This may be inappropriate, but I'm going to say it anyway. When you arrived, Nancy, I thought you *were* Natalie, you looked so much alike. I feel envious when I watch the beautiful open relationship between Natalie and her father. I had that kind of relationship with my father. I wonder if there is any connection between you and your father and Carl?" "That's it!" Nancy sobbed, acting as though she had been struck by a bolt of lightning. She collapsed into herself, weeping her heart out. Between sobs she said, "I didn't really cry at all at my father's death. . . . He really died for me long before his death. . . . What can I *do*?" People responded that he was still part of her, and she could still mourn for him. Ann, who was near her, embraced and comforted her. After quite a time she quieted down, and then in an almost inaudible voice, asked Carl if she could hold his hand.

He reached out and she came across the circle and fell into his arms and her. whole body shook with sobs as he held her close. Slowly she felt better and sat between Carl and Natalie, saying to Carl, "And you look like him too, but I never realized *that* was what I was feeling."

As the three sat there with their arms around each other, someone remarked on how much alike Nancy and Natalie looked. They could be sisters. Carl said, "Here we are, sitting for a family portrait." Nancy said, "But they'll ask 'Why is that girl in the middle sitting there with such a big smile on her face?'" and the incident was rounded off as the whole group joined in her sparkling laughter of release and relief.

CARL'S COMMENTS, LATER

I was very much involved personally and emotionally in this incident, which has, I believe, been quite accurately described. I have also thought about it much since. It is temptingly easy to diagnose the causes of it: Nancy, repressing her pain at losing her father, and seeing a good daughter-father relationship, projects her pain onto Natalie, first by distorting an incident so she could be angry at Natalie, then distortedly expressing her pain through anger at Natalie's close relationship with another woman, and so forth. To me such "explanations" are irrelevant. However, when I try to view it from another perspective it exemplifies many aspects of the existential dynamics of change in personality and behavior.

1. It shows clearly the depth to which feelings can be buried, so that they are totally unknown to the owner. Here it is particularly interesting because it was obvious to Nancy and to the group that she was feeling *something* very deeply. Yet she was clearly labeling it in ways that were not truly meaningful. The organism closes itself to the pain of recognizing a feeling clearly, if that would involve reorganizing the concept of self in some significant way.

2. It is a splendid example of how the flow of experiencing (Gendlin's concept) is used as a referent for discovering the felt

meaning. Nancy tried on the various descriptions and labels that were given to her and they did not "fit." Did not fit what? Clearly, it is some ongoing organismic event against which she is checking. But when Ann pointed—by telling of her own feelings—at another possibility, Nancy realized *immediately* and with complete certainty that *this* was what she was experiencing. It *matched* what was going on in her. As is so often true when a person is acceptantly understood, she was able first to experience the feeling fully and clearly in her sobs. Then she was able to follow her experiencing further, and to realize that in addition to the envy, she felt much pain, and that she had never mourned for her father, because for her he had died years before his death.

3. To me this is a very precise example of a moment of irreversible change, the minute unit of change that taken with other such units, constitutes the whole basis for alteration of personality and behavior. I have defined these moments of change in this way. When a previously denied feeling is experienced in a full and complete way, in expression and in awareness, and is experienced acceptantly, not as something wrong or bad, a fundamental change occurs which is almost irreversible. What I mean by this last term is that Nancy might, under certain circumstances, later deny the validity of this moment and believe that she was not envious, or not in mourning. But her whole organism has *experienced* those feelings *completely*, and at most she could only temporarily deny them in her awareness.

4. We see here an instance of a change in the way she perceives herself. She has been, in her own eyes, a person with no close relationship to her father, unmoved by his death, a person who did not care. Quite possibly she has also believed she was guilty because of those elements. Now that facet of her concept of self is clearly changed. She can now see herself as a person wanting very much a close relationship with her father, and mourning the lack of that as well as his death. The almost inevitable result of this alteration in her self-concept will be a change in some of her behaviors. What those changes will be can only be speculation at this point—possibly a change in behavior toward older men, possibly more open sorrow over other tragedies. We cannot as yet know.

5. It is an example of the kind of therapeutic climate in

which change can occur. It is a caring group, a group that respects her worth enough to listen to her intently, even when such listening breaks into the "task" on which the group was working. They are trying very hard to convey as much understanding as they can. Ann's realness in exposing her own feelings is an example of the openness and "transparency" of the group members. Thus all the ingredients for growth and change are there, and Nancy makes use of them.

6. It is exciting evidence that this growth-promoting climate can evolve, even in such a large group. Sixty-nine people can be therapists, perhaps even more effectively than one, if the group is trustworthy, and if the individual can come to *realize* that and to trust their caring, their sensitive understanding, and their genuineness.

To me it is a small gem—personally meaningful in my experience, but also rich in theoretical implications.

8

Experiential Focusing and the Problem of Getting Movement in Psychotherapy

EUGENE T. GENDLIN

I want to make my main topic the troubles we have when we work with people who do not all explore themselves and their experience. Do you know what I mean? Therefore, I only briefly summarize some more general work already written, for those who do not know it. I want to tell you that early on I did some research and found that for most any orientation of therapy those patients (or clients or people or whatever you call them) who come out changed and satisfied are the ones who during therapy work inside themselves with something that is more than they understand—something they can feel, but do not yet understand. This makes people use odd verbalization. People talk about "heavy feelings" or "being all tied up this way" or "having that funny feeling that other way." They talk about stuff they can feel that does not make sense yet. That is different from emotions; everyone knows what they are. It is different from saying, "I'm mad at so and so for doing this and so."

What I feel but do not yet understand I call a felt sense or a felt edge. It does not yet make sense. By the time it does next week, I will be to a new felt edge.

The statistics of my research showed that those who often during interviews worked with a felt sense had the successful outcomes. This is what I had predicted. It shows that effective therapy is a process of focusing on predefined felt edges. But, we also found that whether the people in these tape-recorded therapies were successful or not could be predicted from the second interview! This upset us very much. We researchers-therapists thought that *we* got people to do this wonderful thing, and now it turned out that that was not so. Those people who knew how to do this when they first came in became success cases. Those who did not know how to do it eventually became failure cases no matter how many years they went to therapy. The finding showed that we therapists did not over time enable them to do it. This was contrary to my prediction and subjective conviction. It was one of those times when one is most glad to have done research. Much research is done to prove something to colleagues. Once in a while it teaches one something and corrects subjective convictions that were really biases. We had to retool and ask the question: "How can we get people to pay attention to their unclear felt experiencing, if they're not already doing it? Is there a kind of teaching, pushing, arguing, pleading, which will get people to turn their attention in this way to the felt edge?"

Now, it is common in our field to talk about getting in touch with feelings, but what I am talking about is different. First of all, it is different because mostly to get in touch with feelings puts one in touch with the feelings that one already knows. Let me stop for a second now and ask you, "If you got in touch with your feelings this minute, what would they be?" I think the ones you just found are already familiar to you. You may be just as well off not getting in touch with those again, because you have done that often enough. Instead of that, what is important is to get a sense of where you are stuck, a sense of the frontier. The felt edge is a sense of the *whole* problem. Getting a felt edge is a different approach than the usual one of going to a familiar bad place and then being stuck there. It is a standing back from that and getting a more holistic sense of what the unresolved whole feels like. That is something which at first feels unclear.

One of the functions of a therapist, in my opinion, is to help the person to stand being at that unclear spot there. Anyone can tell their problem as far as they know it. Then they get to the edge and stop because they canot say anything further. It is not clear there. People think they must be clear. So they run away from the edge. They say something else, they change the subject, they go around in circles, repeating what they do have clear. The therapist must say, "O.K., now we've heard that, now let's stop and stay here, at the edge." There is a slowing down and staying, which is necessary.

You will notice that all the things I have to say are cross-orientational. Helping the person stay there is necessary and possible in Freudian or Rogerian, in Jungian or in any other method. It may be a client or you, working on your own troubles. Slow down and stay with that murky, fuzzy edge of your problem just beyond the point where it is clear.

The second thing is in a friendly way to welcome whatever feeling comes, to receive how it makes a feeling kind of sense. To say, "Oh,yeah, right, yeah, that's the way that feels." If it is someone else you are working with, do that for them. You can say, "Oh yeah, I get that, yeah, oh sure, yeah, right, sure, *scared*." Partly that helps one to stay with it, but it is also an inward processing. "Yeah, right, scared." There is an inward corroboration, over and over, almost like you might do with a child. I urge you to do that also in yourself, with yourself, when you are working on something. This inward processing is usually missed, because our tendency is to zip right past, "O.K., I see what the trouble is, I am scared. Now, why am I scared?" To go so fast skips the body change, the body processing, which we want. The "scared" just came, "Oh, O.K., that's what it is, yeah, right. Can I still feel that again, oh yeah, that's right, scared. Do I really feel

that? Oh yeah, right, there it is." If you do that for about a minute
a body process happens. *Then* you can go on to the next step and
say. "O.K., now, let's see, what's so scary here?"

And by that means, hopefully, the third thing that happens
is that it changes, it releases, or it opens. There is a kind of relief, a
shift, and you go, "Ahhhh, yeah, right *that's* what it is, that's the
scary thing." It is not the information you get that I am emphasiz-
ing, but the body shift. In my opinion the information is not all
that important. If someone had given it to you on a slip of paper
you would have said "that's wrong" or "that's right." Either way
it would not have made a change. It is the body shift that makes a
change, and also it feels good.

One characteristic mark of this focusing process is that it
feels good as a process. You may hate the content, but the steps
feel good. The minute it does not feel good you are not doing it
right; stop, back up an inch, and try to sense why it does not feel
good. The gentle allowing of what is there and the release of a felt
step always feel good.

Now, let me first mention a little bit about the way I use this
focusing in ordinary therapy. During therapy I use it by urging
the person talking to me to slow down. I often say things like,
"Oh, yeah, right," and "Let's stay with that for a minute." I have
many phrases that I use, just to make time so we can slow down.
"Oh, yeah, right, yeah, sure, oh boy, let's stay here for a minute,
let it be, this will change a little later, let's see what it is now for a
while. Sometimes it can take a week to change." I say, "Let's stay
here a while, this may take a while, let's just stay with this, let's
camp here, pitch a tent, get a mattress, build a fire, and just stay
here, it may take a while for this to move. We can camp comfortably, *not in it* but next to it, or a little ways off, we don't want to
run away so we just stay here." You see what I'm doing? I haven't
said anything. It is always a question of staying here, and after
I've done that for a little bit I may say, "O.K., let's ask this feeling
what it is more. What is really so scary? Or, what is really so
hopeless? Or, what is this really that's making you so angry? Or
whatever is here."

Now, I come to the main topic, which is about when it's difficult, when I have a patient, or a friend, a person who isn't in-
trospecting and isn't going to sense feelings or look for them. The

first thing I do is a very old-fashioned thing that I have newly specified and sharpened. I call it "listening." It used to be called client-centered therapy, but by the time I came to client-centered therapy it was already stylish to do it quite roundly and not to repeat everything all the time. When I first came to client-centered therapy I also thought that repeating things was silly. But in the last 3 or 4 years I have relearned it. Indeed, you should repeat everything. It's the only way to discover that you don't get it. If you really repeat it— I don't mean word for word, but the crux of what somebody means—if you say back to them, "So you're telling me that you're really hurt because she let you down," then a person can say, "Well, not exactly, I'm really upset because she let me down," and you say, "Oh, I see, upset." Then the person says, "Yeah, because so and so and another thing is." Then you say back the other thing, too, exactly. And then the person typically exhales and says, "Yeah." Only at that point has the person been heard. There is a quiet that comes now, because what the person had to say got heard. Usually you don't hit it just right the first time. It takes a kind of a rhythm back and forth: they say, you say back, they correct, you get that, they say one more thing, you get that too, then they go, "Yeah," there is a breath and a silence. In this silence the next thing will come to the person inside. Thus one must not talk back and forth forever, but let that little silence be, once the person feels heard. It has to be very exact, let the person very exactly correct you, then stay quiet once they are heard. It is a new thing, it's called *listening*. Give Rogers (1961) the credit, of course, but it is a newly specific, newly old-fashioned thing. Most of the client-centered therapy I have seen in my many years with it wasn't like that. By that means you can help people come down into their experience who otherwise are not looking into themselves. If you really take what they do say, then they get this little quiet, until the next thing comes.

Now, another thing to know about is that sometimes a person's life has to get better before they are willing really to look at their feelings. I am always very willing to use anything that anybody will teach me, and a lot of people have taught me a lot of things, so I use many different kinds of methods. With one particular client I listened, I also tried to teach him how to focus, which he never would do. Among other things we also worked about five minutes every hour on his situation. I learned from my colleague in operant conditioning that it is quite helpful to make small steps of change in one's situation. If you don't have any friends and you're not going out much, it's helpful one week to make a list of places you might go to. The next week it might be good to go to one place and run away as soon as you get there. Perhaps the third week you actually sit there the entire time, but you don't expect anything to happen. Maybe the fourth week you actually talk to one person and you're very proud because you did that. The fifth week you speak to three people and then after that the last step is to look people in the eyes. That starts the high point in the program.

I find that very useful when I have someone without a good relationship. I did with this client. He went from knowing nobody, to going a few places, to finding somebody, to setting up an organization for people who needed somebody, until finally tons of people came through him looking for people, and his life just went straight up. But as far as focusing, nothing. Listening, I did very well, as I do. One time after about three or four months he said to me, "You know, you work awful hard, the other three guys that I saw just sat there and let me talk." It was clear that I was working hard, but not much else was happening. Every once in a while I would try to show him exactly again how one can pursue a feeling or how one could see what a feeling is. The only thing he knew about feelings was to fall into his bad place and take a Valium. I would say that this falling in is not the only way of relating to feelings, there is this focusing way where you don't get wiped out. You don't fall in, but stand back, and you ask into it. And then one time he came in and he said, "You know my life is getting so good these days that the other morning when I woke up and I realized that I had had a dream and it left me with this funny feeling I actually went to see what the feeling was."

I learned from this that it wasn't exactly that I didn't communicate my message and it wasn't exactly that he didn't understand it, it was a process of accumulating a kind of strength so that he could then turn and be the hunter so to speak and go after the feeling rather than hide from it. And this strength came from first making his life better.

Since that time I feel that I can save myself a little. If I see that it will take a few months, I don't want to wear myself out. I understand now. Let's work from all sides. In working with people's situations as well as feelings we are digging a tunnel from the outside in as well as from the inside out. It goes faster.

Another different thing. You can take anything that somebody says and you can consider it *as if* they had said it in the spirit of focusing, even though they didn't. Now here is what I mean by that. I may say to you, "I had to get up awful early this morning to get here." And I may just say that as something that came to my mind, just to tell you about it. But supposing that we're trying to get me moving in therapy and I say that. Now, you know that I don't mean anything by that. I am not exploring myself. I am not doing anything. I am not moving. I am perfectly stuck. I am only saying this because I don't know what else to say. How can we respond to that so as to make a process happen? I want you to imagine a very good patient who *is* exploring, who *is* pointing inward, and who says, "I had to get up awful early to get here today," as an opener to a self-exploration process. What might such a "good patient" mean? What could this be an opener for? Can you imagine something?

They might be saying, "I am mad at you for making me do that just to get here," or they may be saying, "I am doing that for you." There is a whole interactional family there. Do you sense that family? "I am mad at you, I am obligated to you, you're making me do this, I am doing it for you," all sorts of stuff like that.

Now, there could be another type of thing to which this could be an opener. Let's say it's not interactional. Let's say it's an opener to explore inside, what might it be an opener to? It might be an opener to what getting here means, how getting here is important, how changing or doing something about my problem is important to me. It might be a family like that. Do you know what I mean by a family? I mean a cluster of things we could say in ten different ways. Important to me, it's the thing I have hope invested in, it's my wish to change. All those things are one family about what it means to me to come here.

Well, what else might it be? Suppose it's not those things, suppose it's a beginning of getting into a bad problem of mine. What bad problem of mine might be gotten into by starting that way? It could be it's hard to get out of bed, discouraged, getting up early, a draggy sort of down, depressed, lonely kind of quality. It might have been something like there's this depressed background to my things, it's hard to make myself get up all by myself, alone. From that we might go to what's so heavy anyway for me. Or, we might go into why can't I be sufficient to myself without a relationship. Or, we might go into why do I have to organize the world fresh each morning and then it falls apart again every time I go to sleep.

Now, the typical head trip therapist of any orientation feels that he must pick one of those and say to the patient what it really is, it is this one. Of course that's silly, we know that. Assume instead that we don't know yet whatever it really could be. Of course, if we just let me go on talking, we never will know because I didn't say this thing in the spirit of exploring. But you can get a sense and as the therapist you can deal here with that fuzzy edge I was talking about. You can feel what is not yet defined.

Each type of thing you imagine, keep it open and broad. You can now respond *to this vague feeling* even though the person doesn't have it yet because they're not looking there, they have no vague feeling at all yet, they're just telling you they got up early, that's all. But you can respond, you can say, "So that's a heavy way that you feel about when you first get up in the morning?" Or, you can respond with saying, "So that was hard for you?" or you can say, "So what does that feel like when you first get up?" or you can say, "That feeling that you're putting a whole lot of effort into this, what is that feeling more?" In all these examples what is really talked about is "that." "That" is the felt edge that he has there, but he's not looking at it. I can respond to it without deciding what it is, fortunately. If I had to decide what it is I would get it wrong. The point is to get him to turn around and look at it. So, typically, he will say, "No, it's not hard for me to get up," but he'll look at it maybe for a second. He'll say, "It's more like such and so." Even in my very vague way of phrasing it I expect to be wrong, and I expect to be corrected. What I want him to do is look at "that." Usually, of course, it won't work. It will work only once every ten times a little bit. But I can respond like that to *everything* someone says. It's not hard for me to come right back always just to a "that feeling" behind the sentence. "So there's a whole way there, that you feel, about these things not going so well? So that relationship with that person is feeling heavy is it?" I can respond to a felt sense behind any sentence even though the person isn't looking at any felt sense. Then they can correct me or they can ignore me or they can go on, if they want to. And since I can do that at every point with every sentence, it tends to work.

Did you understand this method? It is assuming, even though you know better, that the statement was said in the spirit of self-exploration, then imagining about two or three ways that it could go just to get a general feel, responding to that general feel rather than to the particular things that you thought of and inviting the person to correct you. In an outline it would look like this:

Step I: Take what the person is saying and imagine, even though you know better, that it is being said in the spirit of self-exploring. In other words, let it be the opener of some sort of chain of steps of exploring some personal problems.

Step II: Get yourself one or two or three different ways that that might be.

Step III: Feel that in a general sort of way together.

Step IV: Respond to "that" by somewhat vaguely saying, "So there is this kind of feeling back there behind what you're saying, isn't there, or else tell me how it is," and let him correct you.

Now let me give you a few examples of what a person might say that get you absolutely frustrated because they don't mean a thing by it. Let us start with an easy one. "I don't care." I can imagine right away how a self-exploring person might be saying, "I have this feeling of not caring, isn't that awful? I wonder what that is?" Wouldn't they be a good patient, if they were doing that? "What is this not caring feeling that I have? O.K., it's discouraged or avoidant!" Now your good patient sits there and works to sense what that is. This patient, of course, doesn't. So that's what I would say back, "What is that not caring feeling, is that discouraged?" I am sure the person would say, "No, it's not discouraged, it's uhhh . . . " And I would have him looking at it, which is what I like.

But let us go on to some more examples. "I don't know." I

might respond by saying, "So there's kind of a confused feeling there?" Or if the patient said, "You're just seeing me that way because it's your value system." I'd say, "And you're pissed at having people push their value systems on you?" These are easy examples of thinking of good patients who are really working on something.

What if they had said, "You know, yesterday I went out to buy shoes and they didn't have the right size." Imagine how a good patient might mean something self-exploratory by that. Unable to stand limits? Blowing up at people, you know, displacing, they're going to tell how they blew up in the store because of some little thing? Now we're ready. We can say back, "So then, when they didn't have what you wanted, that's a pretty crummy feeling, isn't it?" See, what I did there? Then they would say, "No, no, no, not crummy." Then I would get a little moment of looking at. Now let's look at some more statements.

Client: "I don't give a damn."

"You have this feeling of anger at people, or just dullness, or what is that feeling?"

Client: "No, that's not what I meant at all and I don't see any sense in looking further."

"That's a feeling of unwillingness you have there." I mean it, it is, isn't it? I'm not saying it in a tricky sort of way, you feel that unwillingness? The person would say, "Yes," I think. Then I could say, "What is in that, maybe you don't want to look?" and they would say, "Hell, no." And then I might stop. I am not solving this completely. But it is a feeling again. See how everything is a feeling, if I want it to be? And I might say a number of other things. I might say, "Are you not knowing what to say now?" "Is there a feeling of stuck in there?"

Client: "I lost my wallet."

"So what does that make you feel? Crummy about yourself?" which would surely go somewhere if it were even close to right.

Client: "How many miles to the gallon does your car get?"

"About 24 when it's working just right. Why do you want to know?" I take it as a real question so I give a real answer, but then I say, "Why do you want to know?" Then he might tell me back, "Because mine doesn't get that much." Then I might say, "Are things discouraging?" And then he might say, "No, hell, no, what are you talking about, I'm just talking about my gas mileage." I realize that, but still that's what I would do.

Client: "What time is it?"

I'd tell you. Then I might say, "Is it getting long? Are you having a feeling there of not knowing what to do with the time? Is it getting heavy? Are you getting tense? Are things uncomfortable?" And notice I can do any number of those really. I do about two or three in my head and then I say one.

I really want the person to turn and attend to the felt edge. I point with general words, without guessing so specifically that I will get it all wrong. In these examples I went with the content each time, because that is what I am trying to illustrate right now. But in actual practice it would be a toss up. I might go with, "You're mad at me" or I might go with, "That feeling you have there." If I sense it being rational I'd probably go with the first.

What I am trying to show is that there is a simple way of considering almost any statement in terms of a felt edge that it comes from, even though the person is not looking at any felt edge. But it takes being willing to make your language vague. But *referring* to it is different than what most therapists do. Most therapists ask probing questions and do not get anything for them from this kind of person. Whereas I can say, "There is that confused feeling there. There is that discouraged feeling there. There is that sense there of the thing not doing well." Then people will turn and look.

If the person wants to stop, I would honestly respond to the resistance. The human reality should always supercede any method, any technique, anything at all. When it humanly feels like someone is saying, "I don't want to and that's it," then I would just simply reflect that back. "You're telling me you don't want to do that anymore and that's it."

The method does not require strong trust between the two people. But I can sense the thing you said about you. I can say to you, "Pay attention to the way 'that' feels in you." And I often say, "Get that for yourself and don't tell me anything. You can decide later what you want to tell me. Get it for yourself first." This is a way I deal directly with there not being enough trust.

Another thing that is important with people who are not getting anywhere in the usual therapy way is that we should be attentive to positive directions. I know there has been an awful lot said about value systems and how we do not agree on these. But when a person is wrestling with stuff, it is not really so hard to decide what is *a pro-life direction*—that needs to and can always be supported. For instance, last week one of the people I supervise had a tape in which a very discouraged woman said that she was stuck in a bad relationship. Then she also said, "Next September I am going to go to L.A. and then I may actually see what I can do about changing everything." And the therapist said back to her, "Well, what can we do right here and now?" And I said to him, "Not so fast. That was a positive direction." First, we want to say, "Oh, so you're thinking of when you get there, taking your life in your hands, and rearranging it all, and taking charge of it, and making it different, doing something, right?" Then she would have said, "Yeah." And then it needs you to say, "That's great!" or, "It feels good to think of changing it all." Only then, when that life-direction has been heard, say, "*What* can we do now?"

On the tape I heard this positive movement and the therapist sat on it, so to speak. She was trying to push that cart out of the mud and he sat on it and said, "Push me too. Do more, come up with something *now*." And so I said, "You get behind it and you push too." At first let's say, "Yeah, you're really going to do something, maybe next September." When we've got the good of that momentum, in a minute or two, then we can always say, "Is there anything that could feel like that now?" I was not objecting to his content. That is what I mean by positive push.

Another example: A person was talking about homosexual things for some stretch and discovered a masochistic feeling of "I want someone to be mean to me." This was like achieving an insight. The therapist wanted him to go further with that. The patient said, "Boy, you could get killed with something like that," and launched into a discussion of how he was going to be a little more careful now that he saw that he had this circuit. The therapist thought this was defensive and wanted unrealistically to explore masochism. As the supervisor listening, I sensed it as life-asserting positive stuff. The man said, "I am going to take care of myself now that I see that." Maybe there is something left to be explored here, but right now that is positive, that's life assertive, you go with that.

I have one more—very often when we talk about feelings some people can and do become aware of body feelings in the sense of tension in the chest or here or there or somewhere. I have found it helpful to say to people like that, "What does this feeling feel like here?" Or, "Can you move your neck tension to your stomach?" I mean that literally. Tensions can be moved around in the body. If you feel real terrible in your gut, sometimes you can move it to your knee, by tapping or tensing your knee, it gives your gut a rest. The same is true in reverse.

There is a focusing possible right at that point where mind and body are not yet split, a fuzzy feeling of something wrong is mind-body-not-yet-split. Indigestion is already just body, follow me? It may feel very similar to something dreadfully wrong. But it is just body. The tension here in my neck is just body, but if I can get the meaningful feel quality of it, then I may discover, "Oh, yeah, I'm carrying something on my shoulders."

Focusing is the *body sense* of some *meaning*. It is at that point where thinking and body are not yet split. A lady in a symposium in Florida some years ago, when I asked her her feelings, pointed to various body spots and said, "I feel fine here, I feel tense here, and I feel fine here." So what could I do with that? I said, "What does your life feel like?" Then she cried. She said, "Oh the convention is almost over and I haven't met anybody and I am very sad." That meant something more. But at that time I didn't yet know how I could connect those two, now I do. My client has his tension here between his eyes. I tell him to move it to his stomach. Then he immediately feels it as fear and can work with it, ask into it.

FOCUSING INSTRUCTIONS

I would like to show you how I might lead a large group through a focusing experience after talking to them about focusing. It would go something like this.

"Now I would like you to take just a few minutes with me. This is different, I would like you to relax, put those microphones and all that stuff down.

"What I would like you to do is, first off, to say to yourself, 'How are you?' and then please *don't answer* the question. Take a whole minute and see what's there and *let it tell you*, don't tell yourself how you are, let it tell you, just how are you?

(Pause)

"And now if you have found a problem in those things that are there, please don't work on it the way you usually do. Instead call the problem 'that.' Pick one problem, one edge, one something you wish were different. Call it 'all that' and wait for me. It doesn't take long to decide, any one will do . Now decide.

"O.K., now I would like you *not* to go in there and do what you usually do. Instead stand back, *don't go in but don't run away either.* Stand back and let yourself feel what it feels like to have that problem, that whole thing. Don't even say anything about it, just call it 'that.' Say, 'What does it feel like to me to have that?'

(Pause)

"The whole feeling of it should give you some specific feeling quality. Something like heavy or urgent or tense or scary or shameful or icky or funnyor something. Can you have a specific feeling quality for the whole feeling there?

(Pause)

"Be with that specific feeling quality, just be with it, and see what it does. If you lose it, come back around and say, 'What does it feel like, oh, yeah, like that.' Just be with it and see what it does and wonder what it is. *Don't tell it*, just wonder, and be with it.

(Pause)

"If the feeling tells you something right away then say, 'Oh, yeah,' and take it and then ask what 'that' is again. Even if you know, *ask what it is, don't answer.*

(Pause)

"Don't let it be just words, stop, wait, and let words come from the feeling itself.

(Pause)

"O.K., now very gently find a fresh phrase or picture to capture exactly what the feeling is so that you have the feeling and also a phrase that matches it exactly.

(Pause)

"Go back and forth, Is that the best phrase? Does that give you the feeling? Is that what it's called? Go back and forth until they match just right.

(Pause)

"If the feeling changes or it goes another step now that's O.K.

(Pause)

"O.K., now this is 'a place' and you might want to come back to this. You might want to come back here. Once you have a feeling and a phrase that match, it's a kind of place. You can dialogue with this place. You can leave it and you can come back to it. Let's come back to it for a moment. Can you still feel the feeling? Does the phrase give it to you?

(Pause)

"O.K., now I would like for you to do one more thing and then we'll stop. You might have to move your body slightly to do this. When you hear this, you might feel like shifting in your chair, letting your body move a little bit. Ask yourself this question and don't answer the question. As before, let a feeling answer it. Wait a few seconds and see what kind of a feeling comes to answer the question. Ask yourself, 'What would this be like and what would this feel like in my body, if this problem were all completely solved, if it were totally O.K., what would it feel like?'

(Pause)

"Think of this as looking up the answer in the back of the book. Now you have the answer, what the answer feels like. We don't yet know the steps to get there. We don't know quite what's in the way. But *hang on to what the answer feels like.* That's the way it feels when it's solved.

"Do one more little thing, now. While you keep this feeling of 'solved,' let's work backwards from it. From the answer, let's get to what's just in front of it. Ask yourself, 'Can I stay that way? Can it stay all solved?' Don't decide, ask. *And let a feeling come and answer you.* You got it already. Or, say, 'I *can* stay this way, can't I?' A feeling will come.

(Pause)

"Did you get a feeling that came and said, 'No, uh, uh'? Well that's the feeling that's in the way! It knows that's still between you and the 'all solved.' Therefore catch this little feeling that says, 'No, uh, uh.' Turn and say to this feeling, 'Hey, you're the one I want to talk to! *You've* got my answer! I am so glad you came! Welcome.' See what this 'No, uh, uh,' feeling is. Just ask, 'Why not?' and wait. It will tell you. If you lose that little feeling, you can get it to come again. Just pretend and say, 'I can feel all O.K., now, can't I?' It will come and say, 'no.' (Or, if it says 'yes', that's fine.)"

Reference

Rogers, C. R., *On becoming a person: A therapist's view of psychotherapy.* Boston: Houghton-Mifflin, 1961.

9

The Far Side of Despair

JAMES F. T. BUGENTAL[1]

Sidney Jourard (1964) has written several papers about the concept of "spirit" which were sufficient to demonstrate that here was a useful way of giving an added dimension to our thinking about human experience and behavior. I found the concept an important addition to my glossary and used it in a paper in which I examined the nature of being and nonbeing as it is evidenced in the psychotherapeutic setting (Bugental, 1967). In this present paper I want to return to this valuable conception of *spirit* and examine its contribution in another context.

In typical Jourard style, Sid wrote (1964):

I am beginning to believe, on the basis of much evidence, hither-to scattered and from apparently unrelated realms, that *something* in the human organism functions in the manner that poets and preachers have said the soul and spirit function. For the time being, I will include the term "spirit" in my scientific vocabulary and define it operationally, or try to. . . . "Spirit" will be said to be maximal when the organization of the [human individual's] system is optimum, mediating valued and ef-

fective behavioral output. . . . Some assumption such as that of "spirit"
and "inspiriting" is necessary to account for a broad range of
phenomena presently not understood, though reliably observed (pp.
79–80).

Familiar language of a nontechnical kind abounds with
phrases such as "feeling in low spirits," "being dispirited," "hoping to raise his spirits," "she gave a spirited performance," "his
actions were full of spirit," and so on. Clearly, our naive perspective is that whatever our spirit may be, they have so much to do
with how we feel in and about our lives and how we translate
what goes on within us into external actions.

My wife and colleague, Dr. Elizabeth Bugental, and I have
been concerned to understand more about those times of low
spirits which we call depression. It is our impression that depression is a common human experience that comes from various
sources and which leads to a range of disruptions of our functioning. I want to describe some of our hypotheses now and invite
your consideration of their possible usefulness in further studies
and in helping ourselves and others when we are dispirited.

PHENOMENOLOGY OF BEING DISPIRITED

I will, first of all, ask you to join me in getting some subjective awareness of the experience of being dispirited. With this
foundation I will present a hypothesis about the nature of the
spiritedness continuum and its relation to our conduct of our
lives. It is my hope in that segment to further Jourard's intent of
bringing this dimension of spirit into articulation with more
familiar psychological phenomena. Finally, I will suggest some
mental hygiene significances of this way of viewing times of low
spirits or depression.

Now, I want to get under way by bringing to our organismic
consciousness the quality of the feeling of being dispirited. To do
so is very much in the Jourard tradition for approaching an area
of inquiry. Here is what I mean: Recently I pulled out of an old
correspondence file some letters Sid Jourard and I exchanged

when we were first getting to know each other in 1963. I'd like to quote a passage from one of his letters (1963):

I seriously wonder if much of therapy couldn't best be understood in analogy to the "redeemed sinner" . . . who gives testimony on Saturday night at the mission, or at the street corner. . . . In all truth, it makes more sense . . . to regard the therapist as one who has had first-hand experience at being phony, inauthentic, neurotic, etc., but who has been "rehabilitated" or redeemed. . . .

It was typical of Sid Jourard to count himself in on the phenomena he studied or the conditions he undertook to treat. He had little patience with a psychology that pretended to great differences between "us" and "them." He saw our common human plight as the subject matter with which he was concerned, and he believed that what he found within himself was to be made a part of the process, rather than focusing solely on experimental objects (which some psychologists miscall "subjects").

In this vein, here are some capsule descriptions of the kinds of feelings with which I want to deal. These come from people close to me and from my own experience:

I feel depressed: Nobody would miss me if I weren't around. Oh, I suppose it would be inconvenient for them for a little while, maybe, but they'd get over it fast. They'd find someone else. It wouldn't make any real difference if I were gone.

I'm feeling dispirited: I'm so bored with everything. It's always the same old thing. There are no surprises; nothing changes. Just the same routine day after day. Every day is like the one before it.

I'm really down: I'm tired all the time. I don't seem to have an energy. I just want to sleep or to sit around and watch some dumb thing on TV. I don't even want to talk with anyone. It's all too much trouble.

I'm feeling low: Everything I try to do fails. Or it just kind of peters out. Nothing comes of anything I start. I'm just mediocre at everything, can't do anything really well. I'm just one of the mob.

I'm in low spirits: My house is a shambles. I keep starting new projects and leaving them half finished. I have lists of things to do all over the house but I never really complete them. I make one resolution after another but I can't seem to follow through.

I'm depressed: I'm smoking one cigarette after another. And I'm eating too much. I have an urge to spend money . . . to buy all kinds of things I don't even need. I pace up and down. I get dressed to go out and then I don't feel like going. I seem to be constantly moving and getting nowhere . . .

Familiar themes run through these capsules, even though they manifestly focus on different areas of experience. The dysphoric, blue, unhappy tone is characteristic of low-spirited times, of course, but notice, too, how often there is the complaint of lack of energy or motivation, of inability to mobilize oneself to act. There is a recurrent sense of blunted intention, of being stranded on the sufferer's own misery. This is an important element to which we will return.

For the moment let us recognize that these themes are familiar to all of us. Variations in spiritedness are experienced by everyone. It is likely that no one escapes depression just as no one escapes anxiety. That universality does not mean that we are all sick, of course. It does mean that these two emotional experiences—anxiety and depression or low spirits—are parts of the heritage of being human.

Sid Jourard pointed out that all of us vary constantly in what he called "spirit titer" (1964, pp. 80—81). To be sure, different individuals tend to have different usual ranges, but all of us know the low times as well as some peaks. In this chapter I am talking about the low times, the depressed times, as a way of understanding them better and as a way of amplifying our understanding of the phenomena of spirit. Thus I am not talking about a diagnostic category or a disease or abnormality. The experience of being low spirited is completely normal, although at times it may be so prolonged or so complicated by other, intercurrent conditions as to produce an abnormal state of being.

Perhaps it will be useful to offer a rather formal definition of dispiritedness or depression as I am viewing it in this presentation:

Depression or dispiritedness is an emotional state characterized by feelings of sadness, pessimism, and futility. In this state, the person tends to have difficulty in initiating and carrying through courses of action and tends to avoid investment in the acts that are carried out or in the human contacts that occur.

This is a description of a fairly pronounced depressed episode, yet one that still may be within normal limits if it is not long continued or complicated by other emotional distresses, such as marked anxiety or suicidal impulses.

Hopefully at this point we have a degree of subjective appreciation of the nature of the low end of the spiritedness scale and some common conceptual perception of that zone of depressed feelings.

DISPIRITEDNESS AS REDUCED PSYCHOLOGIC FLOW

Now I would like to describe a way Liz and I have begun thinking about the experience of being in low spirits as we see it in our patients and as we observe it in ourselves and our friends. I will not call this a theory. Let us just say that thinking about depression in this way is helpful to us in trying to aid ourselves and others to raise our spirit level reasonably soon and with as much benefit as possible.

We start by recalling the fact that change is a common characteristic of all living things. Our bodies are constantly flowing and evolving: Cells are being replaced, neurons are firing electrical charges (randomly even when not being set in motion by human intention), blood is flowing, and food is ingested, digested, and its residues eliminated. Activity and change are the laws of life.

And, of course, the same is true on the psychological level: Our minds are filled with constant flow of images, ideas, memories, anticipations, and so on—as any of us who has tried to practice meditation knows all too well. Our emotions seldom stay the same but are continually evolving. In relationships we find ourselves sometimes drawing close to others and sometimes pulling away. Here again, activity and change are the nature of the creature.

It is our speculation that when this psychological flow is interrupted to some extent, the person experiences a drop in spiritedness. Conversely, we suggest that *spirited* is a term we use to describe a person whose psychological flowingness is open and unobstructed. As an individual begins to experience increased interference with free inner psychological movement, we think he finds his spirits dropping and himself becoming depressed.

In the realm of our physical bodies we know that any appreciable slowing of metabolism, of circulation, of the digestive and eliminative system, or of any other vital system means illness. Similarly, we speculate, a significant slowing or near stoppage of the psychological processes is a source of serious distress and can lead to emotional illness. An arm that is immobilized indefinitely will lose its strength and wither; a psychological function that is immobilized will do likewise. Depression is the emotional component of such slowing or immobilization. As such it is a distress signal, and it may have a healing function as well.

THE INTENTIONALITY SYSTEM

Let me illustrate how our hypothesis works. I do so in terms of the very important life system which has to do with the path by which an impulse emerges from our subconscious and may eventually be expressed in action and in relationships with other people. There are, of course, other dynamic systems within our mental and emotional living, but only time can permit us to examine this one in sufficient detail to illustrate the nature of spiritedness as we see it.

Imagine a freeway or turnpike segment that serves seven major surface streets in a row. For convenience, we'll call those seven Ash, Beech, Cedar, Dogwood, Elm, Fir, and Gum. Of course, the turnpike extends beyond this segment in either direction, but for now our attention is only on the sequence of these seven entrances and exits. A car can enter the turnpike at any point in this sequence and go for any distance the driver chooses. Within certain limits he can select his speed, and he can leave and reenter at another point if he wishes. The chief limitation on travel along the freeway is that the sequence is fixed: If the driver wishes to enter at Beech and go to Fir, he must go past Cedar, Dogwood, and Elm. If he is going from Gum to Cedar, he must pass Fir, Elm, and Dogwood.

There are certain questionable parallels between this geographic turnpike and the freeway I am about to describe, but it will serve our purposes for the moment.

The psychological turnpike or freeway segment I want to imagine now has seven points in a sequence, and we will call these *intentionality, wish, want, will, action, actualizaiton, and interaction.* Let me recognize immediately that each of these words has a long history in psychology which may confuse our communication. Accordingly, I want to describe how I will be using them in this chapter. In the process I hope to make the nature of what we call spirit more evident.

Now what is it that travels this turnpike? Let us think in terms of impulses. An impulse emerges from unconscious and mysterious sources. It is sent forward as an expression of *intentionality,* becomes conscious as a *wish,* matures into a definite *wanting,* is strengthened as an object of *will,* emerges as an *action* in the outer world, is reinforced in *actualization,* and eventually impinges on someone or something in *interaction.* On the other hand, a *wish* may be transformed into a *wanting,* but never gain the support of being *willed.* At other times, an *interaction* may set in motion a sequence that threatens our *actualization* habits, causing us to take counter-*actions* and perhaps to change the thrust of our *will,* even though our *wishing* and *wanting* may remain the same. In other words, impulses may enter our conscious system at any point and move for varying distances in either direction—or even an occasion in first one direction and then the other.

Now I want to examine each of these points on our psychological turnpike more closely. Rollo May, who has written about *intentionality* (1969) more fully and more searchingly than any other current psychologist, says,

By intentionality, I mean the structure which gives meaning to experience (p. 223) . . . I believe that it is also the key to the problem of wish and will (p. 224) . . . Intentionality is the bridge between these [the subjective and the objective]. It is the structure of meaning which makes it possible for us, subjects that we are, to see and understand the outside world, objective as it is. In intentionality, the dichotomy between the subject and the object is partially overcome (p. 225).

Intentionality, we are proposing, may usefully be thought of as a preconscious process that gives the person orientation or direction, which thus is the basis of selective attention and inattention, which makes the person's experience always meaning-filled. One is not conscious of his *intentionality* as such; indeed, it would be not great distortion to say one *is* his *intentionality*. Impulses emerge in the service of the *intentionality*.

By *wish* we refer to a subjective experience of visualizing an object of desire—which may be a thing, a place, an activity, a subjective experience, a relation with another person. We feel an impulse toward making that object a part of our life in some way. A *wish* is a relatively passive experience, without any necessary expectation of fulfillment or perhaps even impossible of fulfillment ("wishing for the moon") (c.f. May, 1969).

When a *wish* becomes a *want*, we are entering the realm of the possible. As our friend Bill Bridges remarks (1976), the good fairy in the stories always grants three wishes, not "three wants." A *want* is something I let matter to me; it is not just the musing of an idle moment. My visualization of a *want* brings it much more into my prospective life, although it still may be held there somewhat tentatively. A *want* is in some measure supported by my determination, my intent for my future.

When I *will* something, I have made a kind of commitment to myself. This is the last, purely subjective step. It is at the threshold of the outer world. What I *will* is definitely in the range of the probable, at least as far as I can see it. I have included the object of my desire in my anticipations for myself. Within the limits of my potency in the realities of the external world. I am going to bring about what I have chosen.

The initial external step we are calling *action*, but it is important to recognize how we are using that word. By *action* we mean taking whatever initiatory step or steps are required to set about bringing the object of my intention into my life. This may be securing the desired thing, meeting the person, taking part in the activity, having the experience, or it may mean engaging in contemplation, allowing myself to grieve, going to sleep, or some other much more implicit or unobservable stop. The key element is simply that there has been a change from contemplating what might be to beginning the attempt to make it actual.

We are using the term *actualization* to characterize the translation of one's impulse into a relatively enduring form in the external world. Where *action*, the preceding step, may be momentary and preliminary, *actualization* shows the underlying intention in a more definitive form. Thus it represents greater risk of censure as one discloses one's being to others. The duration need not be extensive by clock or calendar time, but psychologically it is significant. An outburst of anger after much provocation would be an *action* at the fifth level, as we are here conceiving it, but an angry counterattack or a hurt retreat are more *actualizing* of inner impulses.

The final point of our psychological freeway is *interaction*. We are recognizing that in the living person the end is almost always the beginning as well. Whatever we do is apt to impinge on other people and on some aspects of the world. When that happens, we are drawn into further engagement and new impulses are set in motion. *Interaction* points to the continual recycling nature of experience and to the reality that or lives are set in the midst of continual involvement beyond ourselves.

You should recognize that this freeway carries much that is very important in human affairs, much that affects how we experience our lives, much that is profound in its impact on our emotions. To be sure, we have described it in a oversimple way so far. We have spoken as though there were but a single car on the freeway at a time. Of course, that is never so. Often it is rush hour and the traffic is heavy in both directions. Moreover, any one impulse is not neatly at just one place at a time. Rather it is as though each important set of impulses in our lives is a caravan of cars of related people—say, a bunch of friends on their way to a party on Fir. Some parts of the caravan are already at Dogwood when others are just turning onto the freeway at Ash, while other parts are at various locations in between. So it is with many impulses of our lives. We *want* a new car and much of the impulse is at the *wanting* level, but some element of the feeling is little more than a *wish* and we're not sure whether we're just daydreaming. The old car starts slowly on a cold morning, and the TV ads that night feature just the model we've imagined as having and an important part of our *wanting* has become a *will* to have that car. We visit showrooms, teasing ourselves forward toward *action*, but still with a significant amount of our feelings back only at the *wanting* stage. Then the price of our chosen model shocks us into withdrawing almost totally to the *wish* level. Six months later we see a slightly used car at a great savings and suddenly that *wish* escalates rapidly through *wanting* toward becoming *willed*. We take the car out for a trial run with a friend hoping through this *actualization* to draw the rest of the determination to complete the impulse and enter into the *interaction* of making the purchase.

Spirit, we think, is the dynamic principle that moves our impulses from their germination in intentionality toward realization. Spirit is the power of being, reaching forward into becoming.

DISPIRITEDNESS AND INTENTIONALITY

Now, how does all this relate to what happens when a person is dispirited? It is our hypothesis that depression is the feeling one gets when there is a tie-up on the freeway. On the psychological freeway we have been just describing as well as on the freeway where we drive, things get in a snarl sometimes and then traffic cannot flow smoothly. Depression is one of the emotions that occurs when that snarl severely slows up our internal traffic of intentionality, wishes, wants, willed intentions, actions, actualizations, and interactions. And, just as on actual turnpikes, the longer the tie-up persists, the more traffic and the broader the area affected.

It will aid understanding of our conceptual model if we now describe some of the circumstances that seem to be associated with tie-ups at each of the points in the sequence. It is our hypothesis that each depressed person will show his own unique pattern of inhibitions in this series. That is, Jack Smith may show greatest difficulty in willing his intentions into action, whereas Betty Jones can't seem to find any real wants of her own, and Ted Brown just can't seem to risk genuine interaction with others.

When a person is not able to find a sense of his own *intentionality*, he is apt to be apathetic and, especially in more extreme instances, so withdrawn as to be diagnosed as "catatonic." *Intentionality* blindness, as we may think of it, is a major crippling of the life force and evidences the lowest spiritedness levels. Of course, many of us have difficulty in dependably and fully knowing our own life orientation at particular junctures, and at such times we are often ineffectual and even self-defeating. Yet when such times are relatively infrequent, we are not disabled in life. *Intentionality* blindness or semi-blindness seems often to be associated with schizophrenic disorders and, as such, may derive from early security and relatedness traumata.

The person who is unable to get in touch with his impulses at the *wish* level is handicapped in finding the deeper roots of his own thrust into life. *Wishes* come from the same primitive source as fantasy and dreams and they express much that is unconscious to us. Knowing one's *wishes*, allowing them to emerge freely into awareness, and of course, distinguishing them from other levels of experience, importantly contributes to our feeling of vitality in our intentions and *actions*.

It is important to distinguish *wishes* from other levels of experience I mentioned. I did not say that we needed to distinguish our wishes from "reality," although that would be a more usual admonition. The point is: *Wishes* are real, very real, at their level of experience. When we dismiss them as unreal, we confuse ourselves and often cut ourselves off from an important influence affecting our lives and feelings. *Wishes* are real in the internal world of our experience. Sometimes parents do not realize how important that fantasy-*wish* level is, and they teach their children to shut it off. Sometimes in later years—for example in a science curriculum in college—the person learns to distrust and deny his *wish* impulses. However this comes about, it is a loss to the whole life of the person when he cannot allow himself to know his spontaneous *wishes* so that some of them can become *wants*.

The *wanting* level is the source of awarenes about one's immediate situation. *Wanting* is more conscious and less primitive than *wishing*. It is the level at which we sort out the invitations from the outside and compare them with the promptings from the inside (Bugental, 1976a and b). Advertisements, teachers, politicians, learned books, ministers and priests, authorities of all kinds tell us what we should think and do. If the *wanting* function is crippled, we are at the mercy of the outside. As the Pearsons (1973) have pointed out, if we listen for the internal "hum" in choosing what we will eat, we are apt to have few dietary problems. The difficulty, they say, is that too often we attend to what beckons to us—that is, to what is in the refrigerator or on the menu, to what others say is good, or to the clock and to the calendar. We don't listen to our own *wanting*, and we eat too much, too often, of the things we don't really want. And this same truth holds in other realms than food. When we don't really know our own *wantings* in the moment, we are pushed toward *action* by all sorts of influences and have no reliable way of sorting them out.

In our culture, many of us have learned to mistrust our *wantings*. We have been told:

You can't just think of what you want; remember there are other people too.

If you just pay attention to your wanting, you will be selfish, and no one will like you.

Don't listen to your wanting; it will probably be for bad things, like sex or hurting people.

If you let yourself know your wanting, it will hurt too much if you don't get what you want.

It's all very well to want things, but this is a real world and you'd better listen to those who know what's best for you.

And so on. There have been so many ways we've learned to mistrust our *wanting*, and the result has been that we've been blinded in one of the natural ways of guiding our lives.

Don't misunderstand; I am *not* saying that one should act on all of his *wantings* or that we should only pay attention to our own *wantings*. What I am saying is that our *wanting* is an important, one of the very important, parts of how we choose to live. The person who does not have access to his *wanting* is prone to periods of depression when he realizes how much he is subject to all kinds of influences and how little he finds completion and satisfaction in what he does. Such people may have active fantasy lives with many *wishes*, but their *wishes* have no access to their *wills* and so remain unrealized.

The *willing* function is largely not a conscious one. We sometimes—usually when we have had a struggle beforehand—become conscious of exerting our *will*, but for the most part it is an implicit matter. It is important to recognize that by "will" we do not mean what Rollo May (1969) calls, "Victorian will power" (p. 181). Will power is a very conscious effort to force ourselves in some way—usually against our own *wanting* and in ways which we resist. As we are using the word *will* we are referring to the inner moment of decision which selects from all the *wants* we have those which we intend to make actual. The image I get is that of a mob pressing for entry at the gates of a city, while the guards select a few to admit. The function of will is to act as guards at the gates of *action*.

The person who has difficulty in asserting his *will* is often one who is fearful of conflict. He tends to be indecisive, postponing commitments, and dreading taking a definitive stand. Often he has had a parent who was brutal in overriding his choices or in ridiculing his efforts toward autonomy. The depression which accompanies the suppression of the *will* is frequently characterized by fantasy-wishes for violent action, directed against the self or against others, as the stopped-up *wishes* and *wants* press against the gates that deny them. This can be a very difficult type of problem to work with in psychotherapy, since the person has difficulty in making the commitment to psychotherapy, such a commitment being in itself a volitional step (Bugental, 1976b).

The fifth phase in our sequence is that of *action*. Now the person crosses the border from the subjective to the external. No longer is the impulse potential; it is beginning to become actual. As it takes outward form, it has the possibility of being observed, and thus for the *action*-inhibited person there is the feeling of vulnerability. What he thought and fantasied was safe within himself, but now he is disclosed. Now every word, every moment, seems fraught with the likelihood of disclosing to an antagonistic world the whereabouts and vulnerability of the frightened person. People who suffer this sort of *action* inhibition often have had childhood experiences of excessive and unexplained physical punishment and even abuse. They try to avoid bringing attention to themselves by allowing no impulsive or unscreened *actions* to emerge from them.

The blockage of *actualization* superficially is similar to that just described. The difference is that these people do not usually have the history of physical mistreatment; rather, their pain has been more emotional and subjective. Those who have lived highly structured situations in which there are rules for everything one does are particularly prone to suppress their *actualization* possibilities. Often this inhibition is linked with other emotional elements such as feelings of being blame-worthy, of guilt or unworthiness, or an indefinable but basic wrongness. Here is an autobiographical statement from a person who experienced such depression:

For me, depression is always layered over with guilt so that it is almost impossible to get myself to pay attention in anything like a loving or compassionate way to what is going on inside me. An experience with a woman friend in a psychic healing group was very helpful to me in clarifying a period of depression. The group was silent as we were attempting to follow the suggestion to get into a meditative state in which we would feel grounded and centered. My friend, who was the group's guide, led us through several exercises and then asked us to "clear our space," ridding it of "anything which did not belong" there, in order to "become transparent." We all were to keep our eyes closed. Although I tried, I was quite unable to follow this suggestion. I said nothing, but suddenly my friend said to me, "Are you having trouble?" I said that I was, and she asked, "What is in your space?" I replied that I was surrounded with thick, gooey, brown mud. She said, "Exactly, and everything sticks to you. You will have to work to clear out your space."

I felt immediate relief at this calm recognition of where I was. The layers of guilt, self-analysis, explanations, and justifications began to drop away; although they did not all disappear at once by any means. And there I was; damned uncomfortable, but able to recognize myself where I was; stuck in the mud.

Notice the last thing said, "stuck in the mud." That is a neat metaphor for the experience of the person inhibited from *actualization*. He is layered with so many internal concerns that his actions are heavy and difficult. *Actualization* inhibition is the internal apprehension of external censure, attack, or rejection. It is the more submissive stance. At the next point, *interaction* inhibition, we have the more aggressive stance and external concerns.

The person who finds himself troubled and avoidant about relationships is often one who finds greatest security in working alone. He feels vulnerable to others as does the *action*-inhibited person, but he handles this feeling in a contrasting way. He reduces his awareness of others through controlling carefully his *interactions* and finding many ways of avoiding deep involvement with them. He may produce a great deal of work in an assertive fashion which hides from himself and others his need of them. Here is the self-description of a person experiencing blockage at this point:

It seems to me that from my earliest years my parents taught me to be separate from and somewhat suspicious of others. For a variety of reasons, pursuing creditors being one frequent one, mother and dad often instructed me not to answer the questions of strangers, to be guarded with acquaintances, and to let friends know only selected facts about our lives. Then in addition, we moved frequently—I attended eleven schools before junior high—so I had little experience on continued and deep relations until middle teens. Adult years seem to me to have been a very gradual movement toward risking really being with others. I produced a lot of work professionally, but although I frequently was involved with others, it was always under conditions in which I did my actual work as an individual. The years I spent working in a small group were times of gradually learning to let others come closer and affect me. I still remember the occasions on which the group at the office protested and angrily yet gently taught me that my unilateral decisions cut them away from me and hurt both of us.

It was a new experience to let others influence my actions as companions rather than as competitors or judges. It continues to be a new experience, and I can get very furious at times when the old separateness gets invaded in ways I'm not prepared for. Now, of all things, I'm learning to live in a community of eleven adults and eight children, and I'm getting new and powerful further lessons about sharing. It's a tough learning for me, but ever so gradually I'm making it. Depression can come flooding into me at times when I feel that I've lost all my power of choice, that others control me, that I've given up my independence for a little reward. But there are the other times when I can experience companionship in a way I never knew before.

SUMMARY

Dispiritedness is the emotion we experience when we feel blocked in some important degree in the processes by which we translate our inner impulses into actuality in the outer world. Depression is the experience of feeling unable to use our own potentials in ways that will bring about the kind of life ex-

periences we genuinely want. Our spirits drop as an
accompaniment to or a product of our inhibiting the normal flow
of our unconscious *intentionality* into *wishes*, the translation of
some of those *wishes* into a sense of *wanting*, the implicit selection from among those *wantings* of those which will become our
willed intentions, the emergence of those *willed* into *action*, the
actualization of our *actions* in a more committed way of being,
and their involving us in *interactions* with others.

THE OTHER SIDE OF DISPIRITEDNESS

Now it is time to look at another aspect of the experience of
being dispirited. Consider this poem titled, "Dejection: An Ode,"
and written by Coleridge.

> There was a time when, though my path was rough,
>   This joy within me dallied with distress,
> And all misfortunes were but as the stuff
>   Whence Fancy made me dreams of happiness;
> For Hope grew round me, like the twining vine,
>   And fruits, and foliage, not my own, seemed mine.
> But now afflictions bow me down to earth;
>   Nor care I that they rob me of my mirth. . . .

There is something odd about that last line, "Nor care I that they
rob me of my mirth." What kind of dejection is that that ac-
quiesces in its victimization? Here are two other instances of a
related kind:

Carl is a man in his early forties, a teacher, and a very dispirited person.
He tells me at length of his gloomy forebodings, and as he pauses, there
is a momentary smile.

Grace is emerging from a period of being in very low spirits. She has
begun to see the ways in which she gets caught in a repetitive pattern of
relating to men who will disappoint her and leave her depressed. And
she seems to be fighting off this recognition and clinging to her depression.

And here is a more detailed study:

Carrie has a responsible position in an advertising agency. Although she is 37 years old, she has had very few satisfactory close relationships with men or women. The ones she has had were abruptly aborted in ways that have left her unwilling to invest again. In the course of therapy she invests more in a love relationship than she ever has before. The person with whom she is involved is unwilling to become committed to her, but he is also unwilling to end the relationship.

In the course of her therapy Carrie has become increasingly aware of her pervading sense of powerlessness. With a dominant and punishing mother and a passive but controlling father, she learned early to deal with the world by apparent submission, winning the approval of others through gifts, favors, and hard work. Her usual way of dealing with pain and frustration was to be helpful to others or turn her attention to work. But she is in a place now where she is unwilling to use her former ways of suppressing her feelings. That kind of control is no longer enough nor has it been for a long time. She is, therefore, caught in what I call a "vestibule" to a new way of living. But the vestibule is cold and prisonlike . . . there seem to be no exits.

My sense of Carrie is that on some level she is ready for this low-spirited period, and I know that my alliance with her is strong enough to help her through it. Nevertheless, her pain is acute and I can only encourage her to respect what is going on and to keep a minimum essential structure in her life, however woodenly she performs.

For the first time in years Carrie fails to appear for an important meeting at work. She remains in her apartment wearing a torn and dirty robe, takes the phone off the hook, alternately sitting listlessly staring at the wall and agitatedly pacing from one room to the next. She picks up one book after another and is unable to become interested in any of them. She switches on first the radio and then the TV and turns each off again after a few minutes. She picks up the phone to call a friend and puts it down again without completing the call.

Carrie now begins to describe herself to me as "made of steel," as "all stubbornness," as "stiff as a ramrod." She enacts this for me: a set, cold expression on her face and an unrelenting posture. Where before she had been all compliance and softness, she becomes somewhat aloof and even able to inconvenience me somewhat.

In the course of the next few weeks and without any conscious plan Carrie does several things which are extremely unusual for her. She is rude to a repairman who comes to her apartment at an inopportune time . . . . after which she sleeps soundly for the first time in days. She confronts her mother on the telephone and does not even consider calling her back to apologize or soothe. Discovering a faulty mechanism on her automobile she persists in phone calls and personal visits until the dealer replaces it and pays the expenses of her rented car while the repair is being made. She takes an aggressive stand on an issue at work; she refuses a request from a fellow employee to be a co-signer on his loan; and finally she writes a letter to her lover stating on what conditions she will continue their relationship. This, for docile Carrie is an astounding series of actions! Now in her therapy she enters a new period in which she finds access to early childhood memories that have long been repressed and is able to deal with painful thoughts and feelings in a fluid and immediate fashion she has never known before. Although that emotional pain is still very much a part of her life for some time, the depression steadily decreases. Its work of alerting her has been accomplished.

When nearly a year later, Carrie finishes with her therapy, she looks back on that depression as the turning point in her movement toward fuller and more satisfying living.

What we are suggesting is that our usual way of regarding periods of low spirits or depression as something to be gotten rid of or even denied is inauthentic and destructive. This judgment rests on several recognitions: First, as we have just illustrated, there are hints that there are hidden gratifications in depression. Second, it is apparent clinically that the dispirited time may be a way of demanding attention to aspects of our lives which have been too long ignored. Third, there is reason to believe that, at least in some instances, depression serves as part of a healing process.

Despite the fact that our unthinking reaction to the word "depression" is apt to be one of rejection or aversion, persons in psychotherapy who are highly motivated to candid self-exploration will often recognize that the actual, immediate experience of depression is not truly unpleasant. Indeed, they may say that it is "comfortable" or "safe" or even, astonishingly, "pleasant in a secret way." To be sure, depression can, at times, seem agonizing or terrifying, but inquiry at such moments nearly always discloses that the agony or terror are not from the depression itself, but are linked to the threat of what may come about if the dispiritedness does not change or to the pain of self-castigation for not being as one thinks he should be. Both of these sources are secondary or elaborative, it will be recognized.

The "joy of depression" often feels to the low-spirited

person as though it is guilty or shameful. This may be related to the covert feeling of power that depression can give, especially when the person is successfully resisting the efforts of others to "get him out of" his mood. Because depression is frequently linked with feelings of powerlessness, it is easy to see this as a potent side benefit.

We noted above that dispirited times can have an important signaling function. Viewed this way, depression is not something gone wrong. Depression, as a signal, is something right which is occurring. It is a signal that something is not as it should be in some significant part of our lives. The condition about which it notifies us needs our attention. To suppress the dispirited emotion because it is uncomfortable would be as unwise as pasting a cardboard on our instrument panel to cover the red light that tells us the motor is overheating and explaining doing so because the red light is unpleasant to see. Yet all too many of us learned early to cover this emotional signal in ways we would never use with the mechanical one. Sid Jourard makes this same point in his discussion of spiritedness and of transparency:

Doubtless, when a person is behaving in ways that do violence to the integrity of his system, warning signals are emitted. If only man could recognize them himself, and institute corrective action! Then he would live a hundred years. This fact (of warning signals) is capitalized upon by designers of machines; they build indicators which flash lights when output exceeds tolerances or when intakes are outside a specified range. Fuses blow, governors go into action, and power is shut off. "Normal," self-alienated man, however, often ignores his "tilt" signals—anxiety, guilt, fatigue, boredom, pain, or frustration—and continues actions aimed at wealth, power, or normality *until the* machine stops (1964, p. 101).

Our third observation about dispiritedness is that at times it is apparent that a period of depression can serve a healing function. Depression is, if you will, an altered state of consciousness. Often it marks a time when an overly stressed person finally takes occasion to let himself rest emotionally, intellectually, interpersonally, or otherwise. It may, as we saw above, give a kind of disguised power to a person feeling hopelessly impotent in his usual life. For a person with much inhibited emotion—anger, sexual desire, yearning for closeness—a period of low spirits may be a time of coming to terms with his or her own inner impulses. During such times, one may relax some of the censorship that denies to awareness important needs and feelings. Thus the low-spirited episode may make possible greater inner awareness and harmony.

In summary, we can recognize that although depression has a bad name in our culture, perhaps this ill-repute is not truly deserved. It seems a case of guilt by association. We have confused the discomfort of some feelings with the words that they have in our lives. Depression—along with anxiety, grief, and guilt—have too often been treated as "wrong" or unhealthy. They are neither. They are intrinsic parts of the human experience. When they are accepted and understood, when they are incorporated into our total being and worked through, they free us to live more fully, to experience the good times more thoroughly, to know our total natures more authentically (Bugental, 1965).

MENTAL HYGIENE OF LOW-SPIRITED EPISODES

In this final section, I want to offer some suggestions for ways of thinking about and responding to periods of dispiritedness in one's own life or in those with whom one may be relating—as therapist or as friend.

1. *Recognize that periods of being in low spirits are normal.* One need not be anxious or depressed about being dispirited. Such secondary complications distort the signaling value of the experience and make working it through more difficult.

2. *Reduce complicating factors as much as is realistic during the depressed time.* As indicated above, distress over the fact of low spirits is not really appropriate and is usually counterproductive. Similarly, it is useful to reduce outside demands on one during these times. There is important inner work to be done. One needs to get in touch with his intentionality sequence (the turnpike of our earlier discussion) and try to free up blocked areas. Attempts to function in a "business as usual" fashion are only apt to prolong the dispirited time.

3. *"Go with" the depression to the extent that it is realistic.* This is not a license to impose on the other people in one's life. That seldom works very long or very well anyway, because of one's guilt for doing so and because of the counterreactions of those others. What will work is taking time to attend to one's own inner processes nonjudgmentally, inquiringly, acceptingly. We are well advised to be patient with the low-spirited experience. Like a fever, it is signalling that something important to one's well being is going on; moreover it is a part of that important process.

4. *Since the falling off of spirit is a signal, find out what it is pointing to.* It may be any of one's psychological processes; it is usually a damming up or slowing up of some important area that needs to flow more openly. Often, it will have relationship to the intentionality system which I described earlier.

5. *Locate the stoppage and try to prevent a spread to "adjacent" areas.* For example, if one finds it hard to make decisions during such a period of low spirits, he will often discover that functions more "inward," that is, *wishing* and *wanting*, are still available. Using those that are still open consciously and valuingly may help in preventing the spread of the blocking and even contribute to reducing the stoppage. For example, take time to fantasy a variety of *wishes* and to experience the feeling of one's *wanting*.

6. *When using functions more "outward" from the blocking, exercise sensitivity.* In the example above where the *willing* function was the seat of difficulty, the *action, actualization,* and *interaction* functions should be considered the more outer. One cannot live without engaging in such activities to some extent. But during a period of low spirits, it will be helpful to try to get whatever sense is possible of the intentionality roots of one's actions and to exercise caution in making long-term commitments that may encumber or make difficulties when the depressed period is over.

7. *Avoid forcing oneself as much as possible during this time.* There is the ever-present tendency for many people to become an impatient taskmaster coercing themselves as a reluctant slave/worker and disregarding the depression. There are often social rewards for doing so. Nevertheless, such a way of

dividing one's being and not respecting one's own feelings nearly always is destructive and may confuse the growth or recovery process, thus prolonging the dispirited time.

8. *Keep aware of the hidden gratifications of being depressed.* It can provide an excuse for not meeting obligations, a chance to rest from pressures. It is a legitimate justification for spending time on oneself. Yet it can be self-perpetuating if one enjoys only these hidden gratifications. One does well to take time to examine the trade-offs of holding on to the depressed state in contrast to moving on to more spirited living.

9. *Sensitive timing is important.* In all of these suggestions, one needs to feel his way carefully. Depression work, like grief work, is important, and it takes time to accomplish. One needs to find out what one can do at any given point and then do it as well as he can without self-coercion. One may press to get greater freedom, of course but this needs to be gentle and aware pressure.

10. *If it is not complicated by other emotions, the low-spirited time will be only an episode, not a lasting condition.* It will pass. And ultimately the only person who can complicate it is the depressed person himself.

CONCLUSION

These are suggestions in harmony with the sorts of values which Sid Jourard often stressed. As he wrote:

If we treasure health, we have got to redefine the values by which men live—permit people to be themselves, to satisfy more needs and to acknowledge more self than seems presently to be the case. We even have to inculcate the value of being oneself, over and above our role-responsibilities. We have, in short, to re-define normality ... To state the above considerations in terms of the individual, we can say that a man will remain most energetic, most resistant to illness, most creative, when social mores and socialization permit him to acknowledge without shame a broader range of his real self (1964, p. 105).

This has been our intent: to show the way in which our avoidance of nonhedonic emotions, our social rejection of the experience of being in low spirits, has contributed to our emotional and therefore, physical, ill health and to call for a fresh understanding of this emotional experience of depression, an understanding which values what it brings to us. Thus we see the likelihood that men and women can go through a time of dispiritedness, recognize that it is a normal and important signal for attention, and thus move toward becoming more spirited.

In Sartre's *The Flies*, Orestes says to Zeus, "Human life begins on the far side of despair" (1949, p. 123). The far side of despair is only reached by going through the normal experience of depression. He who would avoid this path, avoids his life's truths. We must broaden our conception of normality so that this road to our life's true beginnings is not denied.

References

Bridges, W. E. Personal communication, November 15, 1975.

Bugental, J. F. T. *The search for authenticity: An existential-analytic approach to psychotherapy.* New York: Holt, Rinehart and Winston, 1965.

Bugental, J. F. T. Existential non-being and the need for "inspiriting" in psychotherapy. In P. Koestenbaum (Ed.), *Proceedings of the First West Coast Conference on Existential Philosophy and Mental Health.* San Jose, Ca.: San Jose State College, 1967.

Bugental, J. F. T. The listening eye. *Journal of Humanistic Psychology,* 16, 55–66, 1976a.

Bugental, J. F. T. *The search for existential identity.* San Francisco: Jossey-Bass, 1976b.

Jourard, S. M. Personal communication, March 12, 1963.

Jourard, S. M. *The transparent self: Self-disclosure and well-being.* Princeton, N.J.: Van Nostrand, 1964.

May, R. *Love and will.* New York: Norton, 1969.

Pearson, L., & Pearson, L. R. *The psychologist's eat-anything diet.* New York: Wyden, 1973.

Sartre, J. P. *No exit and three other plays.* New York: Knopf, 1949.

Footnotes

[1] The conceptual structure and many of the illustrative exerpts in this chapter were developed jointly with my wife and colleague, Elizabeth K. Bugenthal, Ph.D.

IV

Expanding
the Frontiers

10

Research Perspectives in the Psychological Study of Experience

LAWRENCE A. ROSINI

*H*umanistic psychological research is often characterized by its experiential orientation, and by its attempt to balance the behavioral emphasis which characterizes mainstream psychological research. What defines "humanistic" research, and for that matter, what defines "experiential" research, is by no means immediately clear. Part of the problem is that there is no single experiential method, topical area of research, or common theoretical stance that can be agreed on as representing humanistic or experiential research; nor are they by any means coextensive forms. Instead, there are traditions rather than one tradition; approaches rather than one approach. Although this is both the strength and weakness of the scientific study of experience and of humanistic psychology, it puts the researcher at a disadvantage when attempting to communicate the precise context in which the research is intended to be seen.

This chapter describes some of the domain of experiential research and provides, however partially, some context for the psychological study of experience. That domain is comprised of a perspective on the human person, on the objectives of psychology and psychological research, and on issues of method which relate to the psychological study of experience.

PERSPECTIVES ON THE HUMAN PERSON

Many experiential researchers have a view of human nature that is rooted more in philosophy, especially existential philosophy, than it is in any explicitly psychological personality theory. Although they assume that human beings are in the proper focus of psychology, writers such as Shlien (1970), Giorgi (1970), Van Kaam (1969), Gendlin (1962), and others derive their fundamental assumptions of the human person from an existential-phenomenological philosophy. In this view the human person is seen as creating and being created through life with other people, and through life as concretely experienced in the world. The person is seen as changeable and changing through these experiences, and therefore is incapable of fixed and absolute characterization or definition.

Giving primacy to the experiencing qualities of the person leads one to emphasize subjective states as they are situationally evoked, the person's ability to choose and reject alternatives that are concretely met, and the processes by which the person finds, makes, and organizes meaning from the world. Stress is also placed on psychological processes such as perception and cognition as they relate to the creation of meaning for the individual person, rather than as functional processes immediately related to behavior, and in the existential perspective personal history is important insofar as it relates to the shaping of immediate experiencing.

Besides this philosophical origin, another source for discovering the personality theory of experiential researchers is in their critique of the natural science research model and the extent to which they are willing or unwilling to accomodate all or part of it in their own research. Because the objectives of psychological research cannot be set without implying something about human persons, these critiques also reveal the human values of those who make them.

Rogers (1961) warns that limiting the focus of research to externally observable events overlooks the important subjective outcomes of human interaction that are essential to understanding people. Such a limitation also contains the possibility of encouraging a dangerous authoritarian relationship between persons based on manipulation and social control. Two implications are present here: that the human person is capable of intending his/her own goals and freely takes chosen steps to achieving them. Mandler and Mandler (1974) reinforce these implications by arguing that the objectification of "research subjects" denies the existence and exercise of their personal freedom. Laing (1971) goes even further in arguing that it is an illusion to see the human person as a complex of "it-processes" that can be discovered by observation and reported on impersonally, because behavior is totally incomprehensible without the experience that mediates it. And Barker (1971/1972) fears the long-range implications of a research that identifies the human person as the "objective indices of his behavior . . . nothing but measured physiological processes" (p. 142); down the road, human beings could lose their experience of themselves as autonomous, responsible, and choosing. The values that seem to emerge most clearly from these thinkers are the individual person's power of self-definition and power of self-determination.

THE OBJECTIVES OF
PSYCHOLOGICAL RESEARCH

Is psychology a behavioral or experiential science? In the past the question has aroused controversy, but increasingly there is recognition that it is both. For behind the first question is another question, "Is the human person a behaver or an experiencer?" It seems a matter of fact that both need to be accounted for, first, in a description of the human person and, second, as an objective for psychological research. Still, the experiential research needs to establish how experience and behavior relate, and how experience can be a proper focus for experiential research.

The Interrelationship of Behavior and Experience

Behavior and experience are interrelated, not disconnected, in human beings. Laing, Phillipson, and Lee (1972) have developed a schema to describe the interrelationship: "In a science of persons," they write, "we state as axiomatic that: a) Behavior is a function of experience; b) Both experience and behavior are always in relation to someone or something other than self" (p. 13). Applying the axiom to interpersonal behavior and experience, they describe experience and behavior as categories of variables that intervene between one another. There is no direct contact between the experience of one person and that of another; it is through the experience of another's behavior that helps shape the person's behavioral response. Thus behavior is in part a function of experience.

The perceptual psychology of Combs and Snygg (1959), and Kelly's (1955) construct theory also account for behavior in terms of the person's experiencing. The former attempt to "understand the behavior of the individual in terms of how things 'seem' to him" (p. 16), and the latter sought to identify constructs that people develop which enable them to "chart a course of behavior, explicitly formulated or implicitly acted out, verbally expressed or utterly inarticulate, consistent with other courses of behavior or inconsistent with them, intellectually reasoned or vegetatively sensed" (p. 9). Although their research is formally behavioral, Thibaut and Kelley (1959) made an explicit assumption that interpersonal interactions are selected from a repertoire of behaviors that seem to be chosen on the basis of personal satisfaction. Thus, whether the focus of psychological research and theory is on the person's experience or behavior, the other dimension is undeniable in a full consideration of the human person.

Some theoreticians describe the research act as originating

within the experience of the research. Heider (1967) begins his psychology of interpersonal relations, not with formal research, but with use of the "unformulated or half-formulated knowledge of interpersonal relations as it is expressed in our everyday language and experience" (p. 14). He calls his work "naive" or "common-sense" psychology. Allport (1955) encourages the development of a psychology that can be discovered by "looking within ourselves, for it is knowledge of our own uniqueness that supplies first, and probably the best, hints for acquiring orderly knowledge of others. . . . It is by reflecting upon the factors that seem vital in our own experience of becoming that we identify the issues that are important" (p. 23).

Thus although those who stress experience do not necessarily disparage a study of human behavior, the preference is to place behavior in the context of the experiencing individual who acts. It is also congruent with this view to begin the research quest with issues and concerns of the researcher him/herself, and to approach them in the spirit of inquiring curiosity. Human experiencing is accessible to psychological research, although the methods by which experience is studied differ from methods used to study observable behavior.

The Meaning of "Experience"

Although psychological research can, and does, proceed on the basis that experience and behavior are linked and that behaviors are mediated between persons through perception and interpretation, it is important to establish, rather than assume, the connection. Gendlin (1962) has developed a theory of experience that relates external events to inner psychological events, arriving at a formulation of the process by which a person creates meaning. In Gendlin's theory, any experience is comprised of a process ("experiencing") and some kind of content ("symbolization"). Experiencing—the process of experience—is the felt, inner flow of concrete, "raw" sensing. It is preconceptual and presymbolic. It is continually present and is influenced by external events. Experiencing is not as yet represented or differentiated for the person and must be symbolized in order to be known at all.

Experience comes about when experiencing is given content.

The content of experience is its symbolization. Experiencing can be symbolized in a number of ways, the most basic one being direct reference. In direct reference, the person attends to or notices the experiencing process. It is through the interaction between experiencing and symbolizing that experience takes place. It is also through that interaction that meaning is created. Meaning, in fact, is defined by Gendlin in terms of the functional relationship between feeling and symbol:

Feelings are "felt meanings" only insofar as they function in such a relationship with symbols. So functioning, their functions are found to be necessary for symbols to "mean." Symbols and felt meaning are really only possible in such relationships. Apart from them it is not clear what a "symbol" is, nor can we call feeling "felt meaning." Necessarily, therefore, such a functional relationship defines "meaning" (p. 110).

In Gendlin's theory, when experiencing is directly referred to, the meaning is only implicitly felt. It is with conceptual, verbal symbols that meaning is made explicit. Conceptualization is the verbal content of experience, which does not, however, exhaust the potential meanings that are present in the experiencing process. Conceptualization verbally portrays experiencing, but any moment of experiencing is capable of endless conceptualizations, of endless representations and specifications.

It is difficult to overestimate the importance of Gendlin's theory for psychological research. He establishes a continuity between the "purely subjective" experience of the person and the symbols by which that experience is communicable to another person. In the psychological study of experience it is crucial to establish that linkage, for it provides an understanding of the way in which a person's experience is accessible to another, and thus accessible for research.

Experience in Social Psychological Research

Experience is not neglected by mainstream, behavioral scientists. According to a review by Sardello (1970b), the personal awareness of the subject is seen as relevant in interviews that verify whether the conditions of the experiment were fulfilled, as posttests for added information, and in verbal conditioning studies to determine whether the awareness of the subject affects outcome. Research in person perception is gradually moving away from an interest solely in interpersonal behavior and in the function of perception and interpretation in the coordination of behavior. More attention is being paid to perception and interpretation as functions in themselves and how they operate toward the creation of meaning (e.g., Hastorf, Schneider, and Polefka, 1970). Heider (1967), for example, stresses the individual's scheme of things as intervening variables in the creation of the percept:

In order to understand the relation between stimulus patterns and phenomena theoretically, to make general statements about it, intervening variables must be assumed. These intervening variables consist of a hierarchy of meanings and evaluations which can be compared to a system of interlocking concepts or schemata. That percept will arise that best fits the stimulus conditions and at the same time this system or schemata (p. 58).

Scientific assumptions and objectives must be carefully attended to when psychologists speak of experience. Even though the words may be the same, the assumptions here are those of a stimulus-response psychology, and the objectives are to understand "meaning" and "evaluation" as functional processes or mechanisms. Thus even the components of experience can be studied as "it-processes" just as can more readily observed behaviors.

Experience in Therapy Research

The relationship between experience and behavior is central to research on personality change in the client-centered tradition. According to a review of that tradition by Shlien and Zimring (1970), in the earliest stage of research the experience of the client was emphasized as providing conditions for personality change. In the next stage, researchers expanded the list of experiential conditions, but behind these conditions was a phenomenological theory of personality that paid attention to "the uniqueness of phenomenal reality; the growth motive of the organism; the nature of the self as construct made up of perceptions and experiences" (p. 40). In the third stage of research, the experiences of both the client and the therapist were taken as conditions for the client's personality change. And, importantly, experience was included with behavior as the locus for that change, in contrast to the earlier stage where the client's behavioral change alone was seen as the important outcome. The relationship between client and therapist was seen to begin a new experiential process within the client. In the final stage of research, the definition of "experiencing" as underlying variable provided client-centered research with a foundation to posit a growth process in which both experience and behavior changed:

This underlying continuum was conceptualized in terms of seven strands of flow: (1) relationship to feeling and personal meaning, (2) manner of experience, (3) degree of incongruence, (4) communication of self, (5) manner in which experience is constructed, (6) relationship to problems, and (7) manner of relating (p. 44).

Each of these strands was constructed as a manifestation of "experiencing," with growth seen on a continuum from fixity to fluidity both in the underlying process and in each of its manifestations.

Experiential research in the client-centered tradition has employed a wide variety of method, much of it similar in its natural science origins to that used in mainstream psychological research. The assumptions of this research are concerned with the development of a healthy personality and the relationship of health to the experiences produced by the person's relationships. One of the objectives of this research is to develop a theory of personality and personality change.

Other traditions that share therapeutic objectives in their research, although they share some assumptions of psychoanalytic and object-relations theories, can be found in Laing et al. (1972), and in Ryle (1975). Laing is influenced by objects-relations theory and existential philosophy, particularly that of Jean-Paul Sartre. Ryle combines object-relations and construct theories.

Experience in Phenomenological Research

Existential-phenomenological psychology represents the

"purest" quest to understand human experience. Whether pursued in the areas of clinical, social, or any other psychological specialty, it represents an attempt to understand experience *as experienced*. Its objective is "above all to be faithful to the phenomenon of man as a human being" (Giorgi, Fischer & von Eckartsberg, 1970, p. xiii). An example of phenomenological research is a study by Van Kaam (1969) that attempts to make explicit the necessary and sufficient conditions of being really understood by another person. Through the course of compiling and condensing numerous reports by persons of their experience of being understood, Van Kaam produced a synthetic statement comprised of descriptive phrases; each phrase containing the possibility of expansion into either richer descriptions or into more rigorous and abstract theoretical formulations. That synthetic, descriptive statement was, in fact, the result of his study:

The experience of / "really / feeling understood" / is a perceptual-emotional Gestalt: / A subject, perceiving / that a person / co-experiences / what things mean to the subject / and accepts him / feels, initially, relief from experiential loneliness / and, gradually, safe experiential communion / with that person / and with that which the subject perceives this person to represent (pp. 336−337).

Adherents of phenomenological research take strong value stands against research methods that promote an external definition and frame of reference for the data collected, and because the research is almost exclusively experimental, of all the approaches described here, it is the least inclined to give an independent status to human behavior.

ISSUES OF METHOD
IN EXPERIENTIAL RESEARCH

Experiential research has been characterized by a flexible, and in some cases imaginative, use of methods. Because phenomena as experienced are not observable by the senses of another, methods other than those appropriate to studying observable phenomena have been developed.

In contrast, the phenomenological psychologist is concerned with maintaining the richness of the subject's experience. To do so a dialogue is set up between them. The reciprocal participation model described by Sardello (1970a) allows for the researcher to have an idea about what is being sought and to have attitudes about it, but in dialogue with the subject he/she participates at parity and in the spirit of mutual exploration. Intersubjective agreement tolerates a difference in perspective, in experience, and in ideas; what is central is that there is an agreement that mutual understanding has occurred. The mutual understanding is sought in reviewing the transcription of the dialogue, and by further tests back with the subject that the research has understood the subject's experience.

Objectivity

Another issue in experiential method is the problem of objectivity. Whether any science of persons—or any science at all, for that matter—can be regarded as "objective" is a good question. The scientist, even as observer, is a responding reactor, a subjective viewer. But Shlien (1970) poses a central question about objectivity: Is it true that "objectivity" is founded in a distance of the observer from the observed, which makes the observer impersonal and constitutes the observed as an "object"? He answers in the negative and argues that the opposite might be true:

It seems quite possible that distance could make for less objectivity, if by that we mean reliable and accurate representation of the phenomenon being observed. Too much distance could only lead to "projectivity," since the original object would be out of sight (p. 112).

Therefore, the person who is closer to the truth is not the person with the most distance, or the most impersonal in attitude; the person closest to the truth is the "best knower." Then the problem becomes whether the person does, in fact, know, whether he/she will tell, and whether he/she has the capacity to describe. This is by no means an easy problem. Persons may report on what they have heard or read but not experienced firsthand, or they may report what they feel expected to report, or, in all sincerity, persons may speak of their experiences with abstractions that have a general, "distant" quality that seems far away from their experiences. The solution to this problem is not so clear. Perhaps it lies in the "art" of the researcher as it does in the "art" of the psychotherapist, to be able to recognize the difference between abstractions and concrete experience. Or, as Shlien suggests, it may lie in the selection of "skillful, intelligent, non-defensive and/or courageous persons who can know experience well and communicate [their] knowledge" (p. 112). Shlien is also interested in the case study as potentially the richest method for psychological research.

Another method of overcoming the problem would be to select as subjects of research those who are close, personally, to the researcher. Here there is already a relationship that allows an assessment of the level of knowledge, of the way the person is able to speak about his/her experience, and where there is a level of trust between them that allows open, reciprocal communication.

The verbal report is the most common way of gaining access to the person's experience, although it is not the only one. Its limitations are well recognized in that one can make explicit the meaning of an experience that in fact has many implicit meanings, leaving the verbal report partial in comparison to the phenomenon being expressed. But, as Shlien points out, this is not the fault of the verbal report so much as it is a difficulty associated with the complexity of any behavior. The other problem is that it does depend on a level of articulateness, of the ability of the person to put to words the inner experiential events. This problem has been approached from two directions: One is to find tools (such as the Q-sort) to simplify manners of expression and give them an applicability among several subjects; the other is to acknowledge the paucity of psychological vocabularies and allow "loose" language gained by verbal reports to provide psychology with an opportunity to expand its vocabulary. Experiential researchers have been willing to allow a multiplicity of descriptive terms, and psychological research has been greatly enhanced for the introduction of once "loose" terms such as "empathy," "positive regard," "congruence," and "growth."

But it is important to continue searching for accesses to experience. Besides language and verbal communication used in interviewing and questionnaires is the relatively untapped area of imaginative self-expression. Olson (1976) has demonstrated the power of the collage to express personal experience and personal history; to that may be added story-telling and the whole range of creative-artistic expression.

Experiential researchers in both the existential-phenomenological tradition and in the client-centered tradition consider themselves humanistic psychologists, and have little if any problem in assigning the description to the other. Yet for all of their similarities there are fundamental differences with regard to the research act. Some of these differences may be, over time, negotiable; others, however, may keep them in distinct and quite separate traditions. In the end what binds them togther is a commitment to developing a humane, and competent, science of persons.

References

Allport, G. *Becoming: Basic considerations for a philosophy of personality.* New Haven, Conn.: Yale University Press, 1955.

Barker, E. N. Humanistic psychology and scientific method. *Interpersonal Development,* 1971/1972, 2, 137–172.

Combs, A. W., & Snygg, D. *Individual behavior: A perceptual approach to behavior* (Rev. ed.). New York: Harper & Row, 1959.

Gendlin, E. *Experiencing and the creation of meaning: A philosophical and psychological approach to the subjective.* New York: Free Press, 1962.

Giorgi, A. Phenomenology and experiential research: I. In A. Giorgi, W. F. Fischer, & R. von Eckartsberg (Eds.), *Duquesne studies in phenomenological psychology* (Vol. 1). Pittsburgh, Pa.: Duquesne University Press, 1970.

Giorgi, A., Fischer, W. F., & von Eckartsberg, R. (Eds.). *Duquesne studies in phenomenological psychology* (Vol. 1). Pittsburgh, Pa.: Duquesne University Press, 1970.

Hastorf, A. H., Schneider, D. J., & Polefka, J. *Person perception.* Reading, Mass.: Addison-Wesley, 1970.

Heider, F. *The psychology of interpersonal relations.* New York: Wiley, 1967.

James, W. *Essays in radical empiricism.* Gloucester, Mass.: Peter Smith, 1967.

Kelly, G. A. *The psychology of personal constructs* (Vol. 1) (1st ed.). New York: Norton, 1955.

Laing, R. D. *Self and others.* Baltimore, Md.: Penguin, 1971.

Laing, R. D., Phillipson, H., & Lee, A. R. *Interpersonal perception: A theory and a method of research.* Baltimore, Md.: Penguin, 1972.

Mandler, J., & Mandler, G. Good guys versus bad guys: The subject-object dichotomy. *Journal of Humanistic Psychology,* 1974, *14,* 63—78.

Olson, E. *The mind's collage: Psychic composition in adult life.* Unpublished doctoral dissertation, Harvard University, 1976.

Polanyi, M. *Personal knowledge: Towards a post-critical philosophy.* New York: Harper & Row, 1964.

Rogers, C. R. *On becoming a person: A therapist's view of psychotherapy.* Boston: Houghton Mifflin, 1961.

Ryle, A. *Frames and cages: The repertory grid approach to human understanding.* New York: International Universities Press, 1975.

Sardello, R. J. A reciprocal participation model. In A. Giorgi, W. F. Fischer, & R. von Eckartsberg (Eds.), *Duquesne studies in phenomenological psychology* (Vol. 1). Pittsburgh, Pa.: Duquesne University Press, 1970a.

Sardello, R. J. The role of direct experience in contemporary psychology. In A. Giorgi, W. F. Fischer, & R. von Eckartsberg (Eds.), *Duquesne studies in phenomenological psychology* (Vol. 1). Pittsburgh, Pa.: Duquesne University Press, 1970b.

Shlien, J. M., & Zimring, F. M. Research directives and methods in client-centered therapy. In J. T. Hart & T. M. Tomlinson (Eds.), *New directions in client-centered therapy.* Boston: Houghton Mifflin, 1970.

Shlien, J. M. Phenomenology and personality. In J. T. Hart & T. M. Tomlinson (Eds.), *New directions in client-centered therapy.* Boston: Houghton Mifflin, 1970.

Thibaut, J. W., & Kelley, H. H. *The social psychology of groups.* New York: Wiley, 1959.

Van Kaam, A. L. *Existential foundations of psychology.* Garden City, N.Y.: Image Books, 1969.

von Eckartsberg, R. On experiential methodology. In A. Giorgi, W. F. Fischer, & R. von Eckartsberg (Eds.), *Duquesne studies in phenomenological psychology* (Vol. 1). Pittsburgh, Pa.: Duquesne University Press, 1970.

11

Some Aspects of Revealingness and Disclosure

FRANZ EPTING, DAVID SUCHMAN

AND EDWIN N. BARKER

The construct of self-disclosure has received considerable attention in the past two decades, largely because of the empirical and theoretical work of Sidney M. Jourard (1958, 1964, 1968, 1971) and his students. In this work the phrase of self-disclosure has been used to describe the tendency of a person to communicate information about himself to someone else. For the most part this work has been based on a self-report rating scale developed by Jourard and Lasakow (1958). This original instrument consists of six categories of personal information or "aspects of self," each of which contains ten statements, so that there are sixty items which can be disclosed. These items are reported by the subject as having been disclosed at some time in the past in differing degrees to five "target" persons. Either conceptualized as an independent or dependent variable disclosure has centered around the nature of the content of these items Jourard presented.

Recently reviews of the research literature have appeared (Cozby, 1973; Goodstein & Reinecker, 1974) that for the most part have been concerned with Jourard's method of assessing self-disclosure. Although providing considerable evidence for the construct validity of the term self-disclosure operationalized in this way, the reviews have noted aspects of disclosure not directly addressed by these studies and suggest that taking these attributes into account might enable a general tightening down of the hypothesized relationships. Particularly troublesome has been the relationship between self-disclosure and mental health or overall adjustment. At the conclusion of their review Goodstein and Reinecker (1974) made a number of recommendations. First, there needs to be some way to take into account that some aspects of the self are more central and important than others and some are more private. In their view self-disclosure should refer only to that which is both central and private. Second, there needs to be some way of individualizing the meaning that the items on the questionnaires have for people. Further along these same lines Bayne (1974) has addressed the question of "does the JSDQ (Jourard self-disclosure questionnaire) measure authenticity?" His contention is that Jourard's theory about the nature of authentic self-disclosure is not likely to be measured by the present set of standard procedures based on the JSDQ. Examining Jourard's theory, Bayne (1974) states that self-disclosure should mean "accurate, deliberate and predominantly verbal portrayal of one's *real* self to others." His criticisms center on the fact that Jourard's instruments do not allow for a way to assess whether an item is a real or false part of the self when it is reported as information disclosed.

In general, Bayne's concerns are in concert with our purposes in this chapter and that is to approach self-disclosure according to what Jourard describes as the authenticity disclosure of the self to others. Although the literature reviews mentioned earlier contain some mention of other measures of self-disclosure that might be able to address some of the qualities which would make them closer to an assessment of authenticity or authentic self-disclosure, there has been no systematic attempt to address this matter.

The purpose of this chapter is to present a line of research carried out initially under the supervision of the third author, which attempts to expand the assessment of self-disclosure in the direction of authenticity. We choose to label this dimension of self-disclosure *revealingness* or *authentic revealingness,* which is defined as being open and true in a relationship to another so that a person is able to know the other's real self. This is opposed to the situation where people are presenting themselves in a false or phony way in order to obscure knowledge about what they are really like—the person is being generally evasive, intellectual or uninvolved (Barker, 1971/1972).

This chapter presents a brief review of the empirical work carried out in order to assess this conceptualization of self-disclosure as authentic revealingness. One of the most significant departures from the earlier concept of self-disclosure is the present authors' emphasis on personal communication as an ongoing process that nevertheless maintains a discernible direction toward or away from the revealing of the real self. In this way authentic revealingness might be conceptualized as a process variable (English & English, 1958) which places this research in the tradition of Rogers (1958), Truax and Carkhuff (1967), and Gendlin and Tomlinson (1967).

This process conception of communication considers several classes of data in addition to the content of a subject's disclosure to given targets. Variables that contribute to the subject's style of communication are considered in addition to the content of his disclosure. Paralinguistic characteristics of actual verbal productions are treated as data sources in addition to the content which subjects communicate. A conceptual framework is offered that extends from a content-specific definition of personal communication as "disclosure" to a process conception of "revealingness."

This review of research dealing with the process of revealingness is presented in three sections. The first section reviews instruments that were developed. The second section deals with studies in which these instruments have been employed, and the final section is concerned with a general discussion and evaluation of the construct.

INSTRUMENTS

The Quinn Self-Disclosure Questionnaire

Patrick Quinn (1965) developed a self-disclosure questionnaire (SDQ) that was directly derived from the Jourard and Lasakow (1958) self-disclosure questionnaire. This questionnaire consists of 20 items taken from two categories (personality and body) of Jourard's six category system. In this technique the subject is asked to respond by circling either a *yes* or a *no* as to whether he would be willing to tell a specified individual in a specific situation the material involved in that item.

Quinn felt that Jourard's instrument left several questions unanswered. The first of these was the relationship between the instructions to the subject and the meaning of the self-disclosure score, Quinn modified his instructions to read "Would you disclose" as opposed to Jourard's instructions "Have you disclosed" this item. This was an attempt by Quinn to bring the disclosure into the present rather than continue with Jourard's emphasis on past disclosures to significant people. The specific content and the number of items endorsed is utilized as the index of self-disclosure. Overall, the Quinn SDQ is an attempt to measure in a more contemporary fashion the disclosure of high intimacy material to a specific target person, in a specified situation. More recently, other investigators have attempted this same type of modification (Weigel, Weigel & Chadwick, 1969) including Jourard (1971). In a recent study by Wilson & Rappaport (1974) the Jourard self-disclosure questionnaire (JSDQ) "scored for anticipated self-disclosure but not for recalled self-disclosure," predicted the observed performance which was frequency of personal discussion in an interview. This is seen as general support for this direction of modifying the JSDQ.

The Green Self-Disclosure Sentence Blank

Ronald Greene (1964) developed a sentence blank technique for measuring self-disclosure entitled the self-disclosure sentence blank (SDSB). The model used for constructing the instrument was Rotter's incomplete sentence blank (Rotter & Rafferty, 1950). The categories for judging the production to the incomplete sentences was an attempt to refine Hiler's (1954, 1959) category system, which was designed to assess willingness to reveal oneself through the use of the Michigan sentence completion test.

The instrument consists of 20 sentence stems that the subject is asked to complete in an open and straightforward manner. The sentences are judged on a 5-step scale ranging from 1, most revealing, to 5, least revealing. Level one is described as follows: reveals basic feelings of a personal, relevant nature about important aspects of his life; whereas level 5 is described as essentially neutral or evasive material. A judging-by-matching procedure is used where a judge compares each of the 20 sentences with examples in a test manual. The index of revealingness, obtained by summing the levels across the 20 sentences, results in a possible range of scores of 20 (most revealing) to 100 (least revealing). Greene (1964) reports interjudge reliabilities of .83, .84, and .91. These correlations were obtained by three sets of two judges independently scoring separate samples of protocols.

This instrument offers a significant departure from the self-report measures mentioned earlier. A score of disclosure is obtained by judging the actual productions of individuals, that is, written responses to the sentence stems. In general, statements that reflect the subject's willingness to share socially unacceptable or disapproved materials such as worries and doubts are scored higher than statements of more socially approved materials. It is interesting to note that this scoring procedure is in opposition to Rotter's conception of the scoring of socially unacceptable responses as indicative of psychopathology (Rotter & Rafferty, 1950).

The Revealingness Scale

David Suchman (1965) developed a scale for the measure-

ment of revealingness in spoken samples of behavior, entitled the
REV scale. Although the REV scale is similar to Roger's "manner
of relating" scale (Rogers, 1958; Walker, Rablen & Rogers, 1960)
and Gendlin's "experiencing" scale (Gendlin & Tomlinson,
1967), it was developed specifically to be useful in laboratory and
field studies of personal communication. Suchman's intent was to
develop a scale that would reflect both the content and style of
communication during a period of ongoing interaction. Samples
of spoken behavior are simultaneously evaluated for language
style, voice quality, and content.

The REV scale is designed to produce finer differentiation at
the less-revealing end of process dimensions than the earlier
scales developed by Rogers and his associates. The earlier
measures were developed from research in psychotherapy, which
typically dealt with higher levels of process than those en-
countered in laboratory or field studies. The focus of convenience
intended for the REV scale is one that will overlap with some of
the material which might be presented in psychotherapy or a personal interview but which could also be used to codify data from
studies in which the subject would not be expected to be com-
municating at a highly personal level.

The scale consists of six rating categories which have been
applied to samples of interview material. The lower levels are
described as indicating productions where the person talks about
external conditions of the world. The higher levels of
revealingness are described as ones in which the subjects express
themselves with self-involvement and feeling. They "express"
themselves rather than talking "about" themselves. The middle of
the scale serves to separate high revealers from low revealers and
is described by subjects talking about themselves without involvement in what they are saying. The person's style is described
as intellectualized, mechanical, or distant. Using four judges,
Suchman (1965) reported interjudge reliabilities ranging from .53
to .76. With more extensive training of judges Suchman (1966)
reported a correlation of .87. All ratings were based on 3-minute
taped interview segments.

The major contribution of this instrument is the attempt it
makes to assess and reflect in a single index the disclosure level of

an individual by considering what is said in conjunction with the manner in which it is produced. An item of high intimacy value discussed in a distant and mechanical manner would not be scored as highly as the same content spoken with more references to self. Keller (1966) adapted the scale levels of this instrument for use in judging the written productions of grade school children.

The Personal Approach Rating Scale

The last instrument to be described is one developed by James Carpenter (1966) entitled the personal approach rating scale. This instrument is designed to assess a dimension with poles labeled personal versus impersonal. This dimension refers to the view or understanding held by one person regarding another. To view or understand another in a personal way is to attribute qualities that are uniquely human in one's description of a person. The person is invested with volitional qualities, thoughts, and actions that are seen to arise from some internal source. In the personal view one offers an anthropomorphic description of the other. The impersonal view of a person describes him in purely objective terms. This description of the individual would include the types of qualities that could be applied in describing almost any other inanimate or static aspect of the environment. Peripheral and external qualities of the person are emphasized. Treating this dimension as dichotomous, the discrimination made here is simply in terms of which of the two poles applies: the personal or the impersonal pole.

Subjects are asked to write either ten or twenty sentences that best describe a designated target person. Through the utilization of the judges' manual, each sentence is labeled as personal, impersonal, or unscorable. The numerical index is obtained by dividing the number of personal statements by the number of personal and impersonal statements, and then multiplying this product by 100. This score gives a quotient referred to as the personal approach score (PAS). A high score reflects the writer's use of an inward, experiential approach to the material. Using three judges, Carpenter (1966) reported interjudge reliabilities of .59, .76, and .92. In comparing scores obtained from judges with criterion scores, correlations ranged from .55 to .94. In more recent work the three-step scoring (personal, impersonal, unscorable) has been changed to a five-step rating scale (Carpenter, 1976).

RESEARCH STUDIES

In this section research which has been carried out using the instruments described above is briefly reviewed. Basically, two types of research techniques have been used. The first is the investigation of effects that various fantasy, situational conditions, and role-playing techniques have on revealingness scores. In these studies revealingness is usually a dependent variable. The second group of studies mainly concerns the characteristics of the interview that influence revealingness. However, these studies also cover the use of revealingness scales for selecting individuals participating in interviews (independent variables) as well as other types of activities and instruments used for evaluating the characteristics of interactions (dependent variables).

THE USE OF FANTASY, SITUATIONAL MANIPULATIONS, AND ROLE-PLAYING TECHNIQUES

In this section, research is reviewed in which the subject is asked to consider a person who could fulfill certain role requirements or someone the subject has actually known who fulfills certain role descriptions. The interest is in assessing the communication that the subject presents to the role figure.

Taking the position that personal knowledge of another gives one power, Quinn (1965) investigated how "closeness" of a relationship and personal power in the relationship affect revealingness. In this study he considered three levels of acquaintance (closeness of relationship), and two levels of potential power. Subjects were asked to consider individuals who fulfill the role requirements of a friend, an acquaintance, and a complete stranger. To introduce the power variable each of these role figures was then described as either having been invested with high or low control over the subject in an hypothetical situation. Responses to Quinn's questionnaire showed that "friend" was disclosed to most and "stranger" was disclosed to more than "acquaintance."

It was reasoned that a friend is disclosed to at the highest level because part of the contractual agreement for friendship is the keeping of information confidential or at least the use of the information in a nonharmful way. The discussion of the finding that "stranger" could be thought of as a safer target than "acquaintance" follows the folklore description of the person who describes the ease with which it is possible to talk to a complete stranger such as a bartender or a stranger on a train. Perhaps this effect is due to the lack of risk involved in this interaction. The acquaintance, unlike the stranger, does have some potential for using the information in a selfish manner and is not obligated to fulfill any contractual agreement for friendship. On the basis of this and other studies reported in this review, Barker (1971/1972) and Suchman (1966) developed a theory of revealingness involving the constructs of emotional risk and personal trust.

Employing a role-playing technique, Greene (1964) had students in English classes enact two role descriptions and then complete the SDSB. One role description pictured a person who could easily express basic thoughts and feelings (the high-revealing role). The other role described a person who does not reveal his basic thoughts and feelings (the low-revealing role). All subjects enacted both roles filling out two SDBSs with the two roles counterbalanced for the total subject pool. Scored in the direction of defensive concealment with a maximum score of 100, the mean for the higher revealing role was 51.55, and the mean for the lower revealing role was 72.40 ($F(1,16)=44.96$, $p < .01$). This difference indicates that the sentence completion technique is sensitive to the intentional revealingness of persons completing the blanks.

In further support of the nature of the effect of confidentiality and good intentions of the recipient of a message is a study of the effect of perceived threat on levels of revealingness (Greene, 1964). In one group (the low-threat group) female subjects were told that the purpose of filling out the sentence blank was to aid the experimenter in refining the instrument and that their protocol would be kept strictly confidential. In the second group (the high-threat group) they were told that the sentence blank was part of a testing program that was being carried out by the psychology department and that the scores would be made available to their instructors and to the school administration. Consistent with the hypothesized direction of means, the high-threat group had a mean of 64.68, whereas the low-threat group had a mean of 56.05 ($t = 2.83, p < .01$).

Investigating the person-perceptual aspect of revealingness using role descriptions, Carpenter (1966) investigated characteristics of human relationships which affect the written PAS. Carpenter reasoned that persons who occupy central positions in the life of another, and who are regarded with affection should be described by personal rather than impersonal sentences. Groups of undergraduate students read three role-figure descriptions and wrote ten-sentence descriptions of the persons fulfilling the role description. The role-figure descriptions were as follows: 1. A person you know well and to whom you are close (personal friend) 2. Someone you know well but whom you do not like (well-known enemy) 3. Someone whom you like but you don't know very well (like acquaintance). It was hypothesized that the personal friend would be described more personally than the other two figures. The personal friend is liked better than the well-known enemy and known better than the liked acquaintance. An arcsign transform was utilized to normalize the proportions obtained in PAS index, and a one-way analysis of variance was performed.

The role title effect was significant, ($F(2,78) = 2.78, p < .01$). For the well-known friend 29% of the scorable sentences were scored personal. For the liked acquaintance 14% were scored personal, and for the well-known enemy, 11% were scored personal. The only significant difference was between the personal friend and the other two role-figures.

In a second study, Carpenter (1966) studied the relationship between PAS scores and the communication of target persons. In this study 40 introductory psychology students listened to taped interviews and then wrote ten-sentence descriptions of the persons being interviewed. Two types of interviews were presented, and the subjects were given two sets of expectations concerning the reason for listening to the interview. Using the REV scale as a criterion, a high-revealing tape and a low-revealing tape were selected. The two sets of expectations employed are as follows. In the instrumental set the subjects were told to look for particular qualities of leadership while listening to the tape. In the noninstrumental set subjects were told to try to get a feeling for and get to know the person being interviewed.

As hypothesized, the high-revealing interview produced more personal statements than the low-revealing interview. This effect was perhaps because the person in the high-revealing interview was presenting more personal information. In this way the high-revealing nature of the interview let the other person see him in a personal way. Also as hypothesized, the noninstrumental set did produce more personal sentences than the instrumental set. However, as indicated in the significant interaction, this effect was mainly accomplished by the low-revealing group. The percentage of personal sentences was 30 for the noninstrumental set and 31 for the instrumental set for the high-revealing group; whereas this percentage for the low-revealing group was 19 for noninstrumental and 7 for instrumental.

INTERVIEW RESEARCH AND OTHER RESEARCH USING REVEALINGNESS FOR SELECTION PURPOSES

This section reviews research investigating the variable of revealingness mainly in interview settings. In these studies the various instruments used to assess revealingness have been employed as dependent as well as independent variable measures. As dependent variables revealingness measures have been used to assess the qualities of ongoing interview interaction, and to measure the reactions of subjects to various aspects of the interview situation after the interviews had been terminated. As independent variables, they have been used as procedures for selecting subjects.

One question that has been posed concerns the relationship between level of revealingness during the interview and the general style or type of interview that is being conducted. Suchman (1965) interviewed ten introductory psychology students using two interview styles. One type of interview (personal) was described as an interview in which the interviewer tried to get to know the subject as well as possible and enable the subject to trust the interviewer. The other type of interview (impersonal) was described as an interview in which the purpose of the interviewer was to collect factual data about the subject. All subjects received both types of interview, and the order of presentation of interview styles was counterbalanced. The interviews were recorded and scored for level of revealingness using the REV scale. Consistent with the hypotheses in this study, the personal interview style yielded a mean score of 3.50, which was significantly higher than 2.50, the mean score for the impersonal style, $(F(1,8) = 13.16, p < .01)$. One possible interpretation is that the trusting manner of the interviewer in the personal interview style produced in the subjects a more open, trusting perception of the relationship, therefore, yielding higher disclosure rates.

In a second study, Suchman (1966) attempted a systematic replication of the interview style manipulation. In this study subjects were preselected using the Quinn SDQ, on the basis of level of disclosure. In addition to assessing level of revealingness with the REV scale, subjects were asked to describe the interviewer using the PAS and were asked to rate the quality of interview using the Barrett-Lennard relationship inventory (Barrett-Lennard, 1959). The results of this study revealed that the interview style effect was replicated. The mean for the personal interview style was 4.04, whereas the impersonal style yielded a mean of 2.18 $(F(1,2) = 22.58, p < .001)$. It is noted that the mean separation between the two groups is even clearer in this second study. The difference in interview style emerged as a main effect for the two other dependent variables. In the personal interview, the interviewer was described with more personal sentences on the PAS. The interviewer was also rated as more empathic, congruent, and so on on the relationship inventory. The preselection of subjects, however, failed to manifest its effects on the dependent variables independent of the other variables.

A study by Greene (1964) examined the relationship between self-disclosure score and psychotherapists' ratings. He found a correspondence between scores on the SDSB and therapists' ratings of the disclosure level of their patients. Thirty male veterans of World War II and the Korean War were assigned to four psychotherapists. The SDSB was completed by these patients as part of the regular testing program of the clinic in which they were being seen for psychotherapy. Their therapists were asked to rate each patient on a five-point revealingness scale. Each point on the scale was defined with a brief description ranging from level one (indicating that the patient was revealing aspects of his personal and private world) to level five (indicating that the patient revealed nothing of his inner life). The data for all four therapists combined yielded a correlation between the SDSB scores and the rating scale of $r = .47$, $p < .01$, $n = 30$. With one of the four therapists excluded the correlation was boosted to $r = .64$, $p < .01$, $n = 17$.

Further support for the SDSB can be found in a more recent study by Greene (1971), where he reported a relationship between self-disclosure on the SDSB and simple visual acuity. He found, however, that total sensory acuity (used in this study as an operational definition of "contact with reality") was shown to depend on both dogmatism and self-disclosure. " . . . self-disclosure and dogmatism interacted on sensory acuity, so that low-dogmatic self-disclosers did significantly better on sensory acuity measures than high-dogmatic self-disclosers" (p. 46). The SDSB also proved to be useful in a study by Graham (1970) reported by Jourard (1971) examining self-disclosure and attitudes toward death. She found death acceptors scored higher on the SDSB than nondeath acceptors. "Those subjects who more fully acknowledged the finality of their own death entered more fully into self-disclosing relationships . . . than subjects who denied the reality of their death" (p. 162).

Further research with tle SDSB is offered by Carpenter (1976) and Freese (1974) in a correlational study of self-disclosure measures and a mental health scale constructed through a composite of ten of the eighteen scales on the California Personality Inventory (CPI). For a group of thirty students Freese reported a correlation of $-.39$, $p < .05$ between the SDSB and the CPI composite scores indicated paradoxically that the lower revealing subjects scored in the direction of greater mental health. Freese then attempted a refinement of the SDSB by selecting the fourteen highest self-disclosures from his total group of eighty-five and then divided the selected group into seven "free" disclosures and seven "need" disclosures. Free is defined in terms of Maslow's concept of growth-motivated persons, and need is defined in terms of Maslow's deficiency motivation. As expected the seven "free" disclosures scored significantly higher on the composite score of mental health when compared to the "need" disclosures. In a more recent study, however, Carpenter (1976) using the SDSB, the Jourard SDQ, and the PAS designed to measure the use of an inward and elaborated view of the other in a description of them failed to show, overall, the hypothesized inverted *U* function between revealingness and mental health assessed by the CPI. Some limited evidence was reported for a linear relationslip using the Jourard SDQ. Carpenter, in addition, reported a negative relationship between the SDSB and several CPI measures of functioning for female subjects.

In another interview study Carpenter (1970) investigated the revealingness manifested during the interchange of mothers with daughters. For this study Carpenter revised the REV scale to produce four different subscales reflecting: (a) risk-value of the content, (b) personal importance of the content, (c) emotional involvement, and (d) the judge's feeling about the speaker's willingness to be known. The subscales were combined for a total score. It was found that both intimacy of the topic being discussed and whether girls were talking with their own mothers or someone else's mother affected this new REV scale score. Higher revealingness was manifested with both own mothers and more intimate material.

Further investigation of revealingness in the interview context was carried out by Haggerty (1964). Utilizing the SDSB as a preselection instrument, females from an undergraduate psychology course were divided into high, medium, and low groups. Following this, thirty-seven of the females were subsequently interviewed by the experimenter. The stated purpose of the interview was for the subject to help the experimenter understand personal interactions. The interviews were recorded for the original

REV scale scoring, and the subjects were asked to complete a modified form of Jourard's self-disclosure questionnaire requiring only one target: their best friend. The subjects also completed a relationship inventory concerning how much they felt understood by the interviewer, and the interviewer filled out a reverse form of this inventory concerning how much she felt that she understood the interviewees. Finally, the friend who was designated as the target on the self-disclosure questionnaire was asked to fill out the questionnaire in a manner that would indicate what items the subject had actually revealed to her.

Haggerty found a significant difference between her three SDSB groups. The high SDSB group yielded a mean of 3.91 on the REV scale, which was significantly different from the median SDSB group, with a mean of 2.87 ($t = 2.60, p < .01$). The high SDSB group was also significantly different from the low SDSB group, which had a mean of 3.18 ($t = 2.16, p < .05$). No differences were found between the low and medium groups. The interviewees' rating of the quality of their relationslip with the interviewer was not related to their SDSB scores, but it is interesting to note that the interviewer expressed the impression that she felt that she understood the interviewees in the high SDSB group more than the medium SDSBs and that she felt that she understood the low SDSBs least of all. Perhaps as Carpenter (1966) noted, high self-disclosing subjects can be seen more personally.

In summary, this study seems to give further information to support the fact that the SDSB is a meaningful selection device for subjects' predispositions on the revealingness dimension. In addition it is interesting to note that the friends' form of the Jourard SDQ and the subjects' rating on that instrument correlated $+.36$, $p < .05$, $n = 37$. There is some indication that the self-reported disclosures do tend to be corroborated. More recently, Skypeck (1967), using grade school children as subjects, and Swenson, Shapiro, and Gilner (1968), using married couples, have also reported evidence to support this corroboration.

In an attempt to evaluate the revealingness pattern of peer interactions in an interview situation, McLaughlin (1965) carried out a study in which both the interviewer and the interviewee were selected from a subject pool. In a procedure similar to that employed by Haggerty (1964), she selected female subjects with the ten highest and ten lowest SDSB scores from a subject pool of 194 students. These subjects were then interviewed by the experimenter and REV scale scores were determined. From each of these two groups of ten, three subjects were selected on the basis of their REV scale scores. This resulted then in three high-revealing Ss and three low-revealing Ss selected by the SDSB as well as the REV scale. These six Ss were McLaughlin's student interviewees. From the remaining subject pool, those subjects receiving the twenty-five highest and the twenty-five lowest scores on the SDSB were selected for the two interviewee groups. This procedure resulted in a 2 × 2 design; high and low interviewers, and high and low interviewees selected on the basis of revealingness scores.

At the end of the actual interviews, which were concerned with the general nature of college life, the interviewees were asked to complete the Barrett-Lennard relationship inventory and the PAS rating. The interviews were also recorded and revealingness scores were determined. On the basis of the REV scale scores the results indicated there was no difference in either interviewee or interviewer characteristics. Failing to reach a significant difference, the mean REV score for the high SDSB interviewees was 2.73, whereas the low interviewees yielded a mean of 2.75. The difference was similarly nonsignificant for the two types of interviewers, with high interviewers yielding a mean of 2.82, and low interviewers yielding a mean of 2.62. In inspecting these scores it appears that the upper levels of the REV scale were never reached in this study.

It is possible that this failure indicates that more attention needs to be focused on controlling the interview situation in order to get effective discriminations on the REV scale. Another factor that may have contributed to the failure to find significant differences here is that by selecting her most extreme Ss as interviewers McLaughlin eliminated extremely high and low SDSB subjects before selecting interviewees. This truncation of the distribution could have been a factor in failing to reproduce Haggerty's (1964) significant differences between SDSB levels. This pattern of results was also true for the scores on the Barrett-Lennard relationship inventory. In line with these comments, it is noted that Jourard and Resnick (1969) found differences in openness between high and low disclosures in an interview situation. Their interviews were highly structured, and the selection of subjects was from the extremes of a large tested population. The literature reviews in this area (Cozby, 1973; [Goodstein & Reinecker, 1974) have frequently noted that high-disclosing behavior in an interview is not consistently related to disclosure level of the subject. Situational factors can very easily affect this relationship.

In examining PAS ratings, however, McLaughlin (1965) did find a significant difference between the two types of interviewers. For the high-revealing interviewers, 29% of the sentences were judged as personal, whereas the low-revealing interviewers had only 15% of the sentences written about them judged as personal, $t = 1.86, p < .05$. In summary, then, it is noted that although the interviewers were not rated differentially by the REV scale there was a perceived difference in terms of how personally they were rated on the PAS.

An additional study using the REV scale and the SDSB is one carried out by Mellers (1965) on self-disclosure and perception of parents. Mellers selected subjects on the basis of their SDSB scores constituting low, medium, and high disclosure groups. She required subjects to fill out a parent evaluation scale designed to test the subjects' perception of their parents as either positive or negative (Cooper & [Lewis, 1962). Through interviews concerning the happiest and saddest experiences in their childhood, subjects were scored for level of revealingness utilizing the REV scale. Mellers hypothesized that high-revealing subjects would be more open to all experiences, (both positive and negative) and would *report* more negative evaluation of both parents. She reasoned that the high-revealing subjects would have had the most positive childhood experiences but would be least defensive about reporting negative experiences. The results of this study indicated no significant differences between the three SDSB groups in terms of their total parent evaluation questionnaires. However, opposite to prediction, she found a significant negative correlation between the parent evaluation questionnaire and the REV scale scores, $r = -.39, p < .05, n = 43$. The high revealing subjects reported *more* positive parental perceptions. This finding, however, is consistent with a recent study carried out by Vargas

(1969), who reports a significant positive relationship between reported positive childhood experiences and rated level of self-disclosure during a short interview. This relationslip also held when the Jourard SDQ was used to assess disclosure.

In a recent study Shulman (1976) also used the REV scale in an investigation of correlates of perceived helpfulness in informal interpersonal relationships. Subjects were divided into a high and low helpful group based on their frequency of being nominated by friends on a fourteen-item sociometric questionnaire. Subjects were then invited to participate in a small group exercise (providing an opportunity to assess their REV level) and completed some rating scales. There were significant correlations ranging from .549 to .420 for ten of the fourteen sociometric items, indicating that those people who were nominated as most helpful were rated as more revealing. There was also a relationslip found, $r = .403, p < .05$, between subjects' REV scale scores and understanding as a responsive style on the Porter counselor attitude scale—a paper-and-pencil self-report questionnaire. Additionally, Shulman constructed an interview analysis scale based on the Porter self-report scale and found a significant inverse relationship between REV scale scores and the evaluative response style, $r = -.49, p < .05$, based on analysis of the taped interview.

DISCUSSION

The measures that have been presented are a self-report questionnaire (Quinn SDQ), an incomplete sentence blank scored for self-disclosure (SDSB), a personal approach scale (PAS), and a process scale for revealingness (REV scale). All of these measures and Jourard's self-disclosure questionnaire perhaps measure different aspects of revealingess. Their structural differences reflect the intention of the authors to broaden the range of situations in which revealingness can be studied. Although the Quinn SDQ retained the self-report format of Jourard's original instrument, an attempt was made to focus the reporting of disclosure on the here and now. In contrast to these self-report procedures, the SDSB and the PAS derive scores from subjects by asking them to produce a written response which is then evaluated. Attention is focused on the subject's written production. Ratings are made of the subject's actual presentations rather than their self-report of former presentations to various targets. The REV scale is used for rating the spoken behavior of the subject. Paralinguistic variables are considered in addition to the criteria used in the written SDSB and PAS. The focus is on the communication of the subject in a verbal interaction. The REV scale is more closely related to the SDSB and the PAS than to Quinn's and Jourard's self-disclosure questionnaires, since the events to be considered are actual verbal productions rather than reports of what aspects of self have been or are available for self-disclosure.

A systematic investigation of the relationships among these instruments was performed by Haggerty (1964). Using a sample of fifteen female subjects, she reports a significant correlation between the REV scale and the SDSB, $r = .54, p < .01$. The REV scale and the SDSB, however, did not correlate significantly with the simplified Jourard SDQ employed in this study, $r = .15$, ns; and $r = .30$, ns. In a more recent study of the relationslip between some of revealingness measures Freese (1974) reported a significant relationship between Greene's SDSB and Carpenter's PAS for his total sample of 85 subjects, $r = .40$, $p < .01$. In subsequent subanalyses the Jourard SDQ was not found to systematically relate to either of the other two measures. The relationship for the total sample is not reported. Carpenter (1970) (in his study of mother-daughter interaction) reports very low but as least marginally significant correlations between his PAS scores and his modification of the REV scale ($r = .30, p < .05$, $r = .29, p < .10$). Offering a more complete and extensive investigation of the material presented by Freese (1974), Carpenter (1976) reports the expected significant positive relationslip between the Greene SDSB and the PAS but not for the Jourard SDQ. Although these patterns of intercorrelations by and large are consistent with the previous discussion of the relationships among these instruments, these investigations cover individually only a fragment of the full intercorrelational matrix for the five instruments being discussed. An investigation of the total matrix of intercorrelations is presently needed in order to empirically assess the structural and conceptual relationships existing among these instruments.

Consistency and Reliability

Another dimension on which all five instruments can be compared is the amount of constraint which the instrument places on the subject's responses. This is a function of the degree of structure of the instrument. In examining the five instruments, it is apparent that the self-disclosure questionnaires are the most highly structured, asking subjects to place numerical ratings in the cells of a grid. The SDSB is more structured than the remaining measures and asks the subject to complete a series of sentence stems. The PAS constrains the subject less than the previous measures by simply asking for sentences that will describe a selected target. The least constraint is placed on the subject by the REV scale, since verbal productions in an interview are the samples of behavior to be rated. The structure, or lack of it, in the instruments and the resulting constraints placed on subjects, produces differing degrees of complexity involved in the judgments to be made by raters in deriving scores from these instruments. The REV scale, at one end of this dimension of structure, places little or no constraint on the subject. The judge is required to assign a rating based on all of the subject's verbalizations in an interview sample. For the self-disclosure questionnaires, at the other end of this dimension, a self-disclosure score can be obtained by simply adding the ratings the subjects themselves have provided for each item. To expand from the construct of self-disclosure to revealingness, it is necessary to make judgements about more complex classes of belavior. This increase in complexity is reflected in a progressive decrease in the reliabilities of the revealingness measures. Presented in the order of their complexity, the median of the interjudge reliability coefficients reported for the three more complex instruments are as follows: REV md. r = .56, PAS md. r = .76, SDSB md. r = .84. These are compared to the reliability of the less complex and more highly structured Jourard SDQ r = .94. It appears then that reliability coefficients tend to decrease as the measures place less constraint on the subject.

However, it is important to note that experimenters using the REV scale have reported much higher correlations approximating

r = .90 by careful training of judges, and the refining of rating categories (Suchman, 1966). Training sessions in which prospective raters discuss the rating categories and practice using the rating scales is required for adequate reliability. This extra time spent in training is the price which must be paid for the use of complex process instruments.

Research Studies

Studies employing fantasy and role playing techniques provide a demonstration of the sensitivity of the revealingness instruments to situational manipulation. The affective nature of a relationship as well as the level of acquaintance have been shown to influence revealingness scores. Perceived intentions of another and expectations involved in a relationship were also effective in altering these scores. Woven throughout these studies are the variables of interpersonal trust and personal risk in determining the nature of a relationship. As was pointed out by Barker (1971/1972), the variable of authentic revealingness was at first simply thought to be a function of a characteristic base level of the person studied and the assumed "closeness" of a relationship. At present, however, it is realized that authentic revealingness is a function of at least four variables: (1) again, the characteristic base level for revealingness of the person but added to this is (2) the topic of discussion's emotional riskiness, (3) the trust of the person in the communication being maintained as confidential, and (4) the faith that the person has in the good intentions of the other person. The studies reviewed here have provided a beginning to the experimental explication of the influence of these variables on revealingness.

The detectable operations of revealingness as a variable were most subtle in the interview studies. One of the clearest effects was the influence of interview style on the level of revealingness in the interview. This effect seemed to be enhanced by structuring the interview and ensuring the consistency of the particular interview style. Most notably these studies provided the initial steps for investigating specific qualities of interviews outside the psychotherapeutic setting. It is one of the bases on which these studies may provide an impetus for further research.

In conclusion, the purpose of this review is to acquaint the reader with the conceptual dimension dealing with the complex of processes called revealingness. Through these studies data have been obtained about a process that had not been accessible to experimental analysis previously. It is hoped that the use of these instruments will enable researchers to more accurately investigate questions like the hereto troublesome relationship between revealingness and personal health. Further, we feel that evidence has been provided here that movement toward measures which attempt to assess authentic revealingness and dimensions of a *real* self (not detectable on the simpler self-report devices) has produced additional understanding of what self-disclosure means. It is hypothesizing that in this way the theoretical formations concerning self-disclosure can be more accurately assessed.

In many ways the research covered here offers a multidimensional approach to disclosure that perhaps can be used to more fruitfully deal with problems in this area. Perhaps combining these single dimensions of personal approach scale (the PAS), projected level of openness (the SDSB), disclosure in processes (the REV scale), and the usual report of items disclosed (SDQ) may, in fact, yield even further gains in this area. A project such as this, however, has yet to be realized.

References

Barker, E. N. Humanistic psychology and scientific method. *Interpersonal Development*, 1971/1972, *2*, 137–172.

Barrett-Lennard, G. T. *The relationship inventory: A technique for measuring therapeutic dimensions of an interpersonal relationship.* Unpublished doctoral dissertation, University of Chicago, 1959.

Bayne, R. Does the JSDQ measure authenticity? *Journal of Humanistic Psychology*, 1974, *14*, 79–86.

Carpenter, J. C. *The construct personal-impersonal.* Unpublished master's thesis, Ohio State University, 1966.

Carpenter, J. C. *Patterns of self-disclosure and confirmation in mother-daughter communication.* Unpublished doctoral dissertation, Ohio State University, 1970.

Carpenter, J. C. *Relationships between self-disclosure and healthy functioning for both sexes.* Unpublished manuscript, University of North Carolina, 1976.

Cooper, J. B., & Lewis, H. H. Parent evaluation as related to social ideology and academic achievement. *Journal of Genetic Psychology*, 1962, *101*, 135–143.

Cozby, P. C. Self-disclosure: A literature review. *Psychological Bulletin*, 1973, *79*, 73–91.

English, H. B., & English, A. C. *A comprehensive dictionary of psychological and psychoanalytic terms: A guide to usage.* New York: Longmans Green, 1958.

Freese, J. J. *A study of self-disclosure.* Unpublished senior honors paper, University of North Carolina, 1974.

Gendlin, E. T., & Tomlinson, T. M. A scale for the rating of experiencing. In C. R. Rogers, E. T. Gendlin, D. J. Kiesler, & C. B. Traux (Eds.), *The therapeutic relationship and its impact: A study of psychotherapy with schizophrenics.* Madison, Wisconsin: University of Wisconsin Press, 1967.

Goodstein, L. D., & Reinecker, V. M. Factors affecting self-disclosure: A review of the literature. In B. A. Maher (Ed.), *Progress in experimental personality research* (Vol. 7). New York: Academic Press, 1974.

Graham, S. *Level of self-disclosure as a variable of death attitudes.* Unpublished master's thesis, University of Florida, 1970.

Greene, R. *A sentence completion procedure for measuring self-disclosure.* Unpublished master's thesis, Ohio State University, 1964.

Greene, R. *Self-disclosure, dogmatism and sensory acuity as they relate: To humanistic concepts of mental health.* Unpublished doctoral dissertation, Ohio State University, 1971.

Haggerty, P. A. *The concept of self-disclosure.* Unpublished master's thesis, Ohio State University, 1964.

Hiler, E. W. *An investigation of psychological factors associated with premature termination of psychotherapy.* Unpublished doctoral dissertation, University of Michigan, 1954.

Hiler, E. W. The sentence completion test as a prediction of continuation in psychotherapy. *Journal of Consulting Psychology*, 1959, *23*, 544–549.

Jourard, S. M. A study of self-disclosure. *Scientific American*, 1958, *198*, 77–82.

Jourard, S. M. *The transparent self: Self-disclosure and well-being.* Princeton, N.J.: Van Nostrand, 1964.

Jourard, S. M. *Disclosing man to himself.* Princeton, N.J.: Van Nostrand, 1968.

Jourard, S. M. *Self-disclosure: An experimental analysis of the transparent self.* New York: Wiley-Interscience, 1971.

Jourard, S. M., & Lasakow, P. Some factors in self-disclosure. *Journal of Abnormal and Social Psychology,* 1958, *56*, 91–98.

Jourard, S. M., & Resnick, J. L. *The effects of high revealing subjects on the self-disclosure of low revealing subjects.* Unpublished manuscript, University of Florida, 1969.

Keller, J. L. *A study of self-revealingness in children's written communication.* Unpublished master's thesis, Ohio State University, 1966.

McLaughlin, H. G. *Interpersonal effects of self-disclosure.* Unpublished master's thesis, Ohio State University, 1965.

Mellers, A. E. *Self-disclosing and the perception of parents.* Unpublished master's thesis, Ohio State University, 1965.

Quinn, P. T. *Self-disclosure as a function of degree of acquaintance and potential power.* Unpublished master's thesis, Ohio State University, 1965.

Rogers, C. R. A process conception of psychotherapy. *American Psychologist,* 1958, *13*, 142–149.

Rotter, J. B., & Rafferty, J. E. *Manual for Rotter Incomplete Sentence Blank: College form.* New York: The Psychological Corp., 1950.

Shulman, D. G. *Correlates of being perceived as helpful in informal interpersonal relationships.* Unpublished doctoral dissertation, Harvard University, 1976.

Skypeck, G. *Self-disclosure in children, ages six through twelve.* Unpublished master's thesis, University of Florida, 1967.

Suchman, D. I. *A scale for the measure of self-disclosure in spoken behavior.* Unpublished master's thesis, Ohio State University, 1965.

Suchman, D. I. *Responses of subjects to two types of interviews.* Unpublished doctoral dissertation, Ohio State University, 1966.

Swensen, C. H., Jr., Shapiro, A., & Gilner, F. *The validity of Jourard's Self-disclosure Scale.* Unpublished manuscript, Purdue University, 1968.

Truax, C. B., & Carkhuff, R. R. *Toward effective counseling and psychotherapy: Training and practice.* Chicago: Aldine, 1967.

Vargas, R. *A study of certain personality characteristics of male college students who report frequent positive experiencing and behaving.* Paper presented at the meeting of the Southeastern Psychological Association, New Orleans, February, 1969.

Walker, A. M., Rablen, R. A., & Rogers, C. R. Development of a scale to measure process change in psychotherapy. *Journal of Clinical Psychology,* 1960, *16*, 79–85.

Weigel, R. G., Weigel, V. M., & Chadwick, P. C. Reported and projected self-disclosure. *Psychological Reports*, 1969, 24, 283–287.

Wilson, M. N., & Rappaport, J. Personal self-disclosure: Expectancy and situational effects. *Journal of Consulting and Clinical Psychology*, 1974, 42, 901–908.

12

Searching for Knowledge: A Research Appraisal

MARY LEMKAU HORN

Corliss Lamont defined philosophic humanism as "a philosophy of joyous service for the greater good of all humanity in this natural world and advocating the methods of reason, science and democracy" (1965, p. 12). My definition of humanistic psychology comes directly from Lamont's, and with this definition I am able to put my psychology into a fundamental and relatively simple scheme of practical therapy, service, and research. These three concepts are difficult to separate, because in doing therapy individually or in group settings I am also providing service to the communities of which I am a member. In serving the university community or the larger community, I am enhancing my counseling skills, and in conducting my research I am using my knowledge of therapy and service and providing conceptual schemes, methodologies, and data that revert back to use in my therapy and service skills. Thus it becomes very difficult to segregate therapy from service, service from research, and research from therapy. In the pages that follow, however, I will try to distinguish research from the other concepts in the hope of clarifying the role of research in humanistic psychology.

Bugental, in defining humanistic psychology, alludes to the role of research in the humanistic movement. He states:

Humanistic psychology has as its ultimate goal the preparation of a complete description of what it means to be alive as a human being. This is, of course, not a goal which is likely ever to be fully attained; yet it is important to recognize the nature of the task. Such a complete description would necessarily include an inventory of man's native endowment; his potentialities of feeling, thought, and action; his growth evolution and decline; his interaction with various environing conditions (and, here, a truly complete psychology of man would subsume all physical and social sciences since they bear on the human experience actually or potentially); the range and variety of experience possible to him; and his meaningful place in the universe (1967, p. 7).

Research is concerned with the social and ethical responsibilities of the humanist. Service is the ultimate ideal of this philosophy. As Lamont (1965) suggests, humanism's social and ethical goal is for the individual to realize his own actualization through working for the good of *all*, which necessarily includes himself and his significant others. We are not only impelled to goodness by self-interest, but by our interest in all people. Our motivations are not only due to Freud's pleasure-seeking and sexual urges or to any single scheme of ego involvements. We are fundamentally both self-serving and altruistic in our motivations. We are ego-involved in our work toward the good of all people. What better satisfaction of individual needs can be had than to work for the fulfillment of all? The working toward humanism's social and ethical goal of service to all people must also be selfish work. To couple social and individual fulfillment of needs is as it should be to the humanist. One of the ways to satisfy this dual set of needs is through research. Our needs include increasing our knowledge about the world and our relationships within it. Humanistic psychologists, because of their felt social and ethical responsibilities, are in an excellent position to increase the body of knowledge that clarifies our meaning.

THE SCIENTIFIC METHOD

The importance of the sciences and the scientific method to contemporary humanism cannot be overemphasized. Lamont (1965) discusses five ways of seeking truth historically—through revelation, authority, intuition, rationalism, and the scientific method. The first four methods, although each having some use in research, are inadequate because they ignore the controlled experimentation and empiricism that is basic to modern science. Of the fifth way of acquiring knowledge, tle scientific method, Lamont writes:

. . . scientific method embodies whatever is valid in past methods and adds its own distinguishing characteristic of empirical confirmation through accurate observation and experiment. It is this quality of modern science that has chiefly accounted for its enormous success in broadening the area of knowledge, accelerating the process of invention, and extending man's control over his environment (p. 196).

The use of scientific method in humanistic research has been questioned by some psychologists. They argue that we cannot use the scientific method for research on qualities such as "experience" or "feeling" or "human motivation" and, therefore, cannot excel in our research attempts. Humanists argue that this is not so, that the subjective can be studied just as can be the objective. Psychologists who are persuaded by humanism represent a current trend in the field away from rigid ideologic positions to more global positions that represent the experience, on a subjective level, of the individual and of groups of people. Bugental clearly describes this trend in his six major differences between the humanistic orientation (subjective) and the orientation of the behaviorists (objective). His list follows:

The humanistic psychologist:
1. Disavows as inadequate and even misleading, descriptions of human functioning and experiencing based wholly or in large part on subhuman species.
2. Insists that meaning is more important than method in choosing problems for study, in designing and executing the studies, and in interpreting their results.

3. Gives primary concern to man's subjective experience and secondary concern to his actions, insisting that this primacy of the subjective is fundamental in any human endeavor.

4. Sees a constant interaction between "science" and "application" such that each constantly contributes to the other and the attempt rigidly to separate them is recognized as handicapping to both.

5. Is concerned with the individual, the exceptional, and the unpredicted rather than seeking only to study the regular, the universal, and the conforming.

6. Seeks that which may expand or enrich man's experience and rejects the paralyzing perspective of nothing but thinking (1967, p. 9).

These statements seem to me to suggest that humanistic psychologists may be forcing a dichotomy in psychology between themselves and the behavioralists. This need not and should not be done. The goals of research are the same—to add to the body of knowledge involving the meaning of life for all people. The difference between research in humanistic and behavioral psychology lies in orientation, rather than in methodology. The difference lies in what problems will be investigated, in what orientation we will use to select our areas of study. We must all be responsible researchers in terms of the scientific method. The humanistic researcher does not yet have the technology and precision of the behaviorist, which perhaps makes our research more difficult to conduct, but surely it does not make it impossible or implausible. Bugental does not suggest that we abandon the scientific method in humanistic research. We can all excel in our research attempts, even though our orientation to problem areas may be different. There are many studies that are clearly humanistic in direction and that are sufficiently rigorous methodologically to add to the body of knowledge of psychology. These studies also lead to more precise methodologies.

The interaction between science and application seems purely sensible to all psychologists. Somehow, if our research is not applicable to the problems of humanity and community, then "science" has no meaning to our lives. Humanistic psychology, is, and must remain, an applied science and art form, else we lose the goal we have sought of service to ourselves and others. Meaning is the beginning of research. Facts come later and are derived from the meaning.

Stan Lynch (1968), in writing of the difference between

those who conduct their research in the laboratory and those who work in the world of the individual and society, and drawing heavily from Bonner (1965), states that:

As a scientific discipline, it seems that psychology can no longer afford to ignore the realities generated in human experience. Far too many times, the man whose behavior it measures so rigorously emerges from the psychological equations not as a joyous and suffering individual, but as a bloodless statistical unit (p. 4).

Bonner laments the fact that much psychological research borders on the trivial because of the insistence on rigorous measurement. He states:

At the same time, the problems of great moment, the anguish of men, their alienation from themselves and the world, their concern with the meanings of life and death, their longings and disillusionments, their loneliness and relatedness, their yearning for expression and self-actualization—these have fallen outside the sphere of scientific investigation. They can neither be defined operationally nor investigated experimentally (pp. 4−5).

Bonner's statement is most disillusioning to students of humanistic psychology, and his final statement must be argued. To define operationally our concepts is a challenging problem, but by constantly building on prior research dealing with such concepts, we cannot help but revise and improve on our studies. We do not do our research in the controlled laboratory setting, but this does not necessarily make it unscientific or impossible to conduct, nor does it mean that the research conducted in the controlled laboratory setting does not add to the body of knowledge in our field. The problems of great moment of which Bonner writes *can* be studied within the sphere of scientific investigation.

Bonner himself concurs when he defines his concept of scientific humanism as "scientific in an accommodated sense" (1965, p. 21). He states:

. . . the progress of science is stifled by the power of an influential dogma. Positivism, old and new, has been an obstacle to man's search behind the abstractions of science to the living human being. In order to perceive man as a living whole, psychology must admit to its calculations an alternative and enlarged criterion of truth, namely, that an event is true because it has been subjectively lived. This subjective criterion of truth depends not on empirical or logical proof but on immediate experience. . . . (pp. 20—21).

In humanistic psychology we have opened up to these facts and have, in the recent past, allowed somewhat less methodologically rigorous research to be undertaken. I am not suggesting that the methodologies are not well thought out or are not scientific; I am suggesting that they differ somewhat in kind because of the subject matter being studied. The knowledge of human experience has been measurably increased through this research. One of the methodological problems in humanistic research is to define operationally our concepts. To research human experience, however, we necessarily use the terminology and methods of that experience itself. Because we believe our subjective experience to be true, such use of it can provide us with the basis for research that can help us improve the human experience. Subjective experience is different for each of us, and consequently, we cannot fit it into rigid models. The models must become more flexible for the humanistic researcher.

These more flexible models do not lack reliability and validity, however. Ethically, the researcher has an obligation to replicate his and others' results. We do not take reliability seriously enough in this regard. All research is questionable, and the researcher is obligated to share his results and his data. This is a basic tenet of the scientific method. Journals and professional meetings serve this function to some extent, but we need to share on more personal levels and in the replications of our studies.

The measure of validity is universal regardless of model. It is the ultimate measure in science and crosses ideologic and methodologic concerns. If a study is valid—if it measures what it proposed to measure—it is valid, regardless of whether it was metered in the controlled laboratory or with an attitude scale or interview in the community.

RESEARCH IN HUMANISTIC PSYCHOLOGY

There are many examples of research in the humanistic

movement that have added to the body of knowledge about subjective experience. They have practical value in that concepts have come from them which have changed and added to our therapies and philosophies of human experience and relationships. The research is based on the scientific method as it has derived from philosophic humanism and has been accommodated to humanistic psychology. The methodologies of these studies do not need defending or excusing; the light they shed on human problems speaks for their appropriateness in the profession.

An example of early humanistic research is the work of Rokeach (1960). It is research dealing exclusively with the subjective, but which has been accepted by social science because of its sound and careful methodology. This work, begun in 1951, was the early breakthrough for humanistic research. Rokeach's adherence to the scientific method and insistence on quality is a good example of all of us.

Research is often based on the characteristics, determinants, and measurement of single beliefs and attitudes, rather than on belief *systems*. Rokeach felt that because of the stress of research on single determinants there was little theory and research about the nature and change of attitude or belief *systems*. In the investigations that Rokeach reports in his book, *The Open and Closed Mind* (1960), the focus is on the belief system as a whole. Rokeach believes that "much of man's social behavior can be better understood by relating such behavior to man's belief systems rather than to the elements of such systems" (p. 19).

Rokeach's concepts were defined in detail and were reliably tested by his instruments. His whole methodology was intricate and well designed. His aim was to develop a way of thinking or a set of concepts through which it would be possible to describe the organization of belief systems and to describe individual differences within the organization of the system.

From my point of view, Rokeach has succeeded in his research goals. With his description of belief systems, it has been possible to investigate many abstract concepts, including mate selection, career choice, prejudice, and religious beliefs. This study is an excellent example of rigorous methodology in the use of the scientific method in psychological research.

Landsman (1961, 1967, 1968, 1969, 1974) has spent many of his career years studying what he describes as the "beautiful and noble person," and what this person has experienced. His taxonomy of experiences (1968, p. 4) has been useful to numerous students of humanistic psychology in their personal lives, their professional work in counseling and psychotherapy, and in their own research. Landsman found, through a careful methodology, that the human relationship experience is primary in the lives of his "beautiful" people. Other experiences he has isolated are conquest, excitement, beauty, completion, earned success, and superhuman relationships. Others have used his taxonomy to begin to look into the effects of different kinds of experiences on human lives. Some of these are turning-point expeiences (Fuerst, 1965), the experience of being understood (Baggett, 1967), negative experiences (McKenzie, 1967; Horn, 1975), the intense experience (Lynch, 1968), the transcendent experience (Privette, 1964), and the relationship of life experiences to levels of functioning (Duncan, 1970; Horn, 1975).

These studies have, for the most part, built one on another in terms of defining concepts to be operational for study and in the methodologies used. It is interesting to note the variety of names used for the person described as productive, efficient, and self-fulfilled (Landsman, 1968) by the researchers of these studies. That person is called "fully functioning" by Rogers (1961), "beautiful and noble" by Landsman (1968), "the disclosed self" by Jourard (1964), and "self-actualized" by Maslow (1962). All these terms refer to the same kind of person. It appears that here is a case in point of the confusion that may result from the humanistic researcher's reticence to strive for commonality in definition. I myself have added to that confusion by calling that person "high functioning" (Horn, 1975).

An example of humanistic research that directly built on Landsman's conceptual scheme, using also the studies of other of his students, is my own research on negative experience and its impact on the level of functioning of a sample of women. I describe the research in some detail to stress that humanistic research can and must have impact for the practical application of helping ourselves and others to enrich our lives. As I have earlier stated, this is one of the goals of humanism and humanistic psychology. Occasionally, we lose sight of the ultimate goal, and our research takes the form of the triviality of which Bonner (1965) writes, just because it can be done with the least resistance. We must undertake research that will lend itself to use in our own lives as well as in the lives of others.

The research outlined here (Horn, 1975, 1976a, 1976b) was concerned with the integration of negative experiences: how, personally, these experiences are handled by the individual. I related these experiences to the development of self-actualizing (high functioning) and non-self-actualizing (low functioning) women. A basic assumption of the study was that experience is indeed related to level of functioning. Already, several problems of operational definition are evident. Some psychologists will balk at even the attempt to define "integration" and "experience." The humanist, on the other hand, can see merit in the attempt, and with the help of many others who had used the concepts, reasonable definitions were written that could be used in the study. If more study were now done, using the same definitions, or building on the basics of them, the concepts would become more valuable to the body of knowledge concerned with functioning.

Each of us makes use of concepts or constructs when we organize our data, so that we can perceive relationships among the data. A concept is an "abstraction from observed events" (Selltiz, Jahoda, Deutsch & Cook, 1961, p. 41). It represents a variety of facts, but subsumes them under one general classification. Some concepts are very closely related to what they represent— the concept "ball" is easily understood by looking at balls, all of which have characteristics in common. Some concepts are not so easily related to the facts they represent. Values, attitudes, experience, the meaning of life, motivation, and integration are concepts that are at higher levels of abstraction from the phenomena that they represent. Selltiz and her colleagues write of such abstractions:

The greater the distance between one's concepts, or constructs, and the empirical facts to which they are intended to refer, the greater the possibility of their being misunderstood or carelessly used, and the greater the care that must be given to defining them. They must be defined both in abstract terms, giving the general meaning they are intended to convey, and in terms of the operations by which they will be represented in the particular study. The former type of definition is necessary in order to link the study with the body of knowledge using similar concepts or constructs. The latter is an essential step in carrying out any research, since data must be collected in terms of observable facts (p. 41).

Our difficulty often lies not in defining the concepts in abstract terms, for those abstractions are generally related to the intuitions we have that result in conducting our research. For example, in my own research I used the vague concept of "integration" or experience into the personality. Giving a general meaning of integration as relatedness or unification was not difficult. But it was also necessary to define it in terms of operations so that data could be collected using observable facts. This was done by breaking down the concept into several different levels so the raters who helped with the study could have a clearer understanding of it. Each level had a precise definition which could be tested.

Operational definitions are adequate if the procedures used to gather the data are good indicators of the concepts themselves. This is often a matter of judgment. Oftentimes, especially in the early study of a problem, the researcher feels his data reflect his concept only in a limited way. The replication of a study can result in more succinct definitions of abstract concepts (Selltiz, et al., 1961).

Self-actualization, or high functioning, was relatively easy to define because of the body of knowledge already existing around these concepts. Maslow (1962), Shostrom (1964), Rogers (1961), Jourard (1964), and Landsman (1968) had previously defined them. There are some differences in the definitions put forth by these writers, however. For example, Landsman's "beautiful and noble person" is a more social being than the self-actualized person defined for Shostrom's personal orientation inventory.

Humanistic research must be concerned with people living in their social worlds and not in the confines of a laboratory. Because of this, the samples of high- and low-functioning women were selected by other people who lived with them in those worlds, rather than by external means. It was a subjective evaluation on the part of nominators from several segments of the community. The nominations were validated by the use of objective testing, but the decisions of the nominators were subjective ones. All the nominator's decisions were validated by tests, which indicates that the careful selection of nominators has validity for sample selection. To be able to cut down on the amount of testing done is important to the researcher in terms of subjects' time. When we use human subjects we are confronted with time and energy problems. To be able to reduce the time and effort put into research by subjects is important to us. Any validation of less time-consuming instrumentation is helpful.

Another example of less usual psychological methodology was in the data collection. I used the structured interview, a technique used for years in valued sociological and anthropological research. To comply with rigorous scientific method, I conducted all the interviews myself, after being trained in interviewing techniques. The interviews were all taperecorded, which by its very nature poses some problems of confidentiality and comfort for the subject. These are certainly not insurmountable and depend, to a large extent, on the skill of the interviewer. Trained evaluators and raters were used to interpret the tapes.

Humanists concerned with research must be *more* skillful and *more* knowledgeable than those doing research in the laboratory. We must be more aware of sound methodology so that, if and when we deviate from it, we build on it, rather than destroy it or use it wrongly. If we are to use the world as our laboratory, and the people who subjectively live in that world, we must know more about it than others. Our backgrounds and educations must be broader and more varied. We must be trained and train ourselves to be more competent than if we were working in the controlled laboratory setting. If we are not, when we deviate even the slightest bit from traditional method, we stand to destroy the scientific method, rather than enhance it. This is true not only in our methods of collecting our data, but also in analyzing it. We must know statistical procedures very well, so that in choosing what we will use, we choose correctly.

Humanists are fortunate in that their broad goals lead them to relationships with many kinds of people who they can draw upon for help. We are encouraged to share by our very philosophy, which puts us in the enviable position of being willing and able to ask for help. Students who are of a humanistic persuasion generally ask for help and teachers of the same persuasion generally give it willingly. Such sharing of knowledge cannot but help in designing sound studies.

I have used this short synopsis of my own research to point to some of the areas in which humanistic researchers may vary from more rigid methodologies but not from the scientific method. The details of this research can be found elsewhere (Horn, 1975, 1976a, 1976b). To continue to use my own research only as an example, I will write of some of the results and their importance to me and my work and to that of some of my colleagues.

When I undertook the research, I wanted to find ways to increase my skill and knowledge in working with professional and career women in counseling, both individually and in groups. I had small samples (fifteen in each group) of high- and low-functioning women. Their functioning was rated both in professional and personal terms. I talked to these women about negative experiences in their lives and how these experiences had affected them and how they had coped with them. Personally, I met some unusually interesting and pleasant women and have enjoyed my contacts with them. Surely humanists can admit to the pleasure they find in conducting their research!

The results of my study were in three areas: integration of negative experience, sources of help, and the subject's present perceptions of her past negative experiences.

In integrating their negative experience, high-functioning women either simply accepted their negative experiences and "went on living" or worked through all the aspects of an experience and made it a part of their life patterns and personalities. This type of woman integrated her experiences highly. The low-functioning group of women did not integrate negative experiences very well. These women tended to concentrate on their problems and negative experiences, and tried to work them through, but were not successful in this process. They did not cope well as a group. For some reason, their negative experiences served to muddle their perceptions and to make their lives more uncomfortable. They were unable to "let go" of past negative experiences. The unresolved negative experiences seemed to be one variable in their lower levels of functioning.

In terms of sources of help, the high-functioning women

used self-help more than they did the help of others. The high-functioning group, as tested, was more innerdirected, more dependent on self, than was the low-functioning group, which suggests that these women would use themselves, their inner resources, for help with their negative experiences. The low-functioning group of women was more dependent on others for support, which suggests that this group might well seek professional help, which was the case.

High-functioning women presently perceived more of their negative experiences as positive ones than did the low-functioning women. They were able, through their coping mechanisms, to turn many of their negative experiences into positive ones. The low-functioning group was less able to do this. There were some experiences (death and rape, for example) that both groups continued to perceive as still negative.

I conducted this research so that I could learn more about some of the people with whom I work. It was humanistic in intent, and as such, must add to my knowledge, and to that of others, in our goal of serving people. Humanistic research *must* add to our knowledge and skill or it has no value to the profession.

Since conducting this research I have changed some of my counseling techniques when I work with women who perceive themselves and who I perceive as low functioning in their professional and/or personal lives. For example, I now try to help women become more self-dependent and independent, because I recognize these as characteristics of more highly functioning women. At one time I may have believed that my client's being more dependent on me might have been helpful to her.

I have also begun to more actively insist that my clients who are generally like the subjects of my research, work on the specific problems that seem to be at least partially responsible for their low levels of functioning. It has been my feeling for some time that women feel an obligation to the "Movement" to talk about the ideologic issues of womanhood, of liberation, of freedom, and so forth, when what they need and want to talk about (not only in therapy) are their own personal problems of disruptive children, career choices for themselves, and so on. They feel some guilt if they concentrate on themselves rather than on all women. My research has been helpful to me in insisting that my clients be more specific in terms of their own personal needs and in helping them to work with the guilt that often ensues.

This research has also been useful in my supervision of students. I am more comfortable in suggesting helpful ways of treatment for women returning to school or work, for vocational counseling for women like those of my sample, and for women who function at low levels within the community.

The research has also been important to me in my personal as well as my professional life. As I have stated above, I found the conducting of the study both pleasurable and enlightening. Since I am a woman like some of those in my sample, I have gleaned insights into my own use of negative experience and level of functioning in terms of my family and professional lives. The study has been useful to me personally, which is one of our goals as humanists.

I, and many of my colleagues, have used the results of this particular research in other and more subtle ways as well. I have used this research only as an example to point out that research in humanistic psychology must have application to our lives. Some of the methodologies of such research deviate from the traditional, but we deal with the subjective, which also deviates from the traditional subject matter in psychology. This, in no way, means that we conduct less rigorous or less meaningful research. We are both scientists and creative artists. In many ways, we are more rigorous and more skillful in our research because we are forced to overcome the sentiment of some that we cannot excel in conducting research. Our research is more meaningful because we insist that it have applicability to the goal of humanism: to serve the greater good of all humanity.

References

Baggett, R. L. *Behaviors that communicate understanding as evaluated by teenagers.* Unpublished doctoral dissertation, University of

Florida, 1967.

Bonner, H. *On being mindful of man: Essay toward a proactive psychology.* Boston: Houghton Mifflin, 1965.

Bugental, J. F. T. (Ed.). *Challenges of humanistic psychology.* New York: McGraw-Hill, 1967.

Duncan, C. W. *A comparison of certain experiences by life stages of selected groups of self-actualized, modal, and low functioning college students.* Unpublished doctoral dissertation, University of Florida, 1970.

Fuerst, R. E. *Turning point experiences.* Unpublished doctoral dissertation, University of Florida, 1965.

Horn, M. L. *The integration of negative experience by high and low functioning women.* Unpublished doctoral dissertation, University of Florida, 1975.

Horn, M. L. *The helping professional and career women: Notes on counseling and therapy.* Paper presented at the meeting of the National Association of Women Deans, Administrators and Counselors, New Orleans, March, 1976a.

Horn, M. L. *Self-actualizing and non-self-actualizing professional women: The integration of negative experience.* Paper presented at the meeting of the Southeastern Psychological Association, New Orleans, March, 1976b.

Jourard, S. M. *The transparent self: Self-disclosure and well-being.* Princeton, N.J.: Van Nostrand, 1964.

Lamont, C. *The philosophy of humanism* (5th ed.). New York: Ungar, 1965.

Landsman, T. Human experience and the human relationship. In *Personality theory and counseling practice.* University of Florida. Materials Diffusion Project, 1961, 42–52.

Landsman, T. One's best self. In S. M. Jourard (Ed.), *Existential psychological studies of the self.* University of Florida Social Science Monographs, 1967, *34*, 37–50.

Landsman, T. *Positive experience and the beautiful person.* Presidential Address, Southeastern Psychological Association, Roanoke, Va., April, 5, 1968.

Landsman, T..The beautiful person. *The Futurist,* 1969. *3*, 41–42.

Landsman, T. The humanizer. *American Journal of Orthopsychiatry,* 1974, *44*, 345–352.

Lynch, S. *The intense human experience: Its relation to openness and self-concept.* Unpublished doctoral dissertation, University of Florida, 1968.

McKenzie, D. H. *Two kinds of extreme negative human experiences.* Unpublished doctoral dissertation, University of Florida, 1967.

Maslow, A. L. *Toward a psychology of being.* Princeton, N.J.:Van Nostrand, 1962.

Privette, P. G. *Factors associated with functioning which transcends modal behavior.* Unpublished doctoral dissertation, University of Florida, 1964.

Rogers, C. R. *On becoming a person: A therapist's view of psychotherapy.* Boston: Houghton Mifflin, 1961.

Rokeach, M. *The open and closed mind: Investigations into the nature of belief systems and personality systems.* New York: Basic Books, 1960.

Selltiz, C., Jahoda, M., Duetsch, M., & Cook, S. *Research methods in social relations.* New York: Holt, Rinehart and Winston, 1961.

Shostrom, E. L. An inventory for the measurement of self-actualization. *Educational and Psychological Measurement,* 1964, 24, 207–218.

Sid Jourard—The Teacher: One Student's Perspective

MARTIN AMERIKANER

*I*n *Healthy Personality*, Sid's most recent book, there is a section entitled, "On recognizing a consciousness larger than one's own" (1974). His description of having an enlarged awareness is an apt summary of what being a teacher meant to him. One person wishing to learn, and another, larger person to act as a guide. Through that complex process of exploration, modeling, and laughter he understood so well, teaching and learning would occur. To those of us who spent time with him, Sid was a teacher.

It had little to do with the time of day or where he was. Unlike so many others, Sid did not need those confirming symbols of the teaching role—the lectern and the office—although he was an excellent lecturer and always took the time to listen to students who came to his office. More than this, though, Sid loved his ideas, and wanted to play with them all the time, whether at school, or at parties, or at lunch, or at the beach. However, this was not the dreaded "talking shop" which fills the emptiness at so many social occasions. No, this was a playful passion, an everpresent component of his grown and growing self. He never tired or grew bored with this aspect of his work—as he refilled everybody's glass once again, he would often say, "One can never have too much wine."

Sid's favorite metaphor for growth was that of the journey— that taking off on a voyage to explore and to discover. For Sid, though, a successful trip included the return home. Go out, come back; go out, come back. This model always struck his large class of undergraduates, since, quite literally, they were on a voyage of discovery up in Gainesville, but whether from Miami or Moore Haven, they would soon have to deal with returning home. However, this metaphor is also useful in describing why Sidney was such an excellent teacher. The return is a time for incorporating the newly discovered with the older, more stable structure; the time for processing those pictures you took on your trip. It is this time of reintegration that defines real growth, and prepares a larger person for the next adventure. Sidney was always out exploring, but continuously integrating too, and thus the home base from which he dove was getting larger and larger. It was this ever-expanding, revitalized center that made him such a vast and readily accessible resource. When he taught an interdisciplinary seminar on man and metaphor, or co-taught a course on behaviorism and humanistic psychology, it wasn't a stab in the dark. He would seek out faculty and students and bring together their varied experience. Together they would explore some new combinations of ideas, integrate what was fruitful, and push on.

Integration and expansion—my thoughts keep returning to these words when I think of Sid's teaching. Self-disclosure. The constant process of revealing one's self, while not getting caught up in openness as an end in itself. Letting himself be known while simultaneously becoming new again.

We would be driving across campus to class, discussing the upcoming lecture, when his head would turn, eyes light up, and, "Isn't she lovely," would emerge. Then back to the topic, never missing a beat. He'd be typing a letter to someone when I might come jumping into the office with some ridiculous idea or a new, profound insight. He would listen carefully, with that amused light in his eye, and somehow find something of value in what I was saying. Then he'd rip it apart, because of X, or Y, or Z, and finally convince me to keep at it, because after all, it was a good idea in the first place. I would drift out, vaguely excited, trying to piece together what had just transpired, while the typewriter was already clacking away once again. One did not easily upset the rhythm in Sid's day.

It was always important to build from something. His view of teaching psychotherapy was the apprentice system; the student would work with an experienced guide, making use of him as a model when necessary, and learning from him all he could; from this the student's personal "style" would emerge. Develop a resource base, then strike out on your own. Similarly, in research the idea was to build rather than poke out blindly. Though some did not consider Sid a researcher, he surely understood the process of science, the cumulative nature of a growing body of knowledge. If I would propose some outrageous, but to me, perfectly reasonable study, the criticism would not be of the idea or question itself. More often, he would comment that I wasn't building on what I already knew; I wasn't using information or methods that had previously proven valuable. By no means was this thinking conservative—rather, he tried to convey that in research, as in all modes of development, real advancement is based on, yet goes beyond, what has already been accomplished.

Sid was a teacher who expected one to do things well, or, as he would say, "Do it magnificently." Undergraduates were constantly amazed that their expected "gut" course in humanistic psychology—that soft stuff—would flip from an easy A to a challenge for Bs and Cs. Students who handed in gibberishladen term papers which they thought sounded nice and "humanistic" would take them home with toughminded comments all over them. It wasn't easy to bullshit old Sid. Yet, those who put care into their work received thoughtful and encouraging criticism. He, not his assistant, read and wrote comments on every paper, and this was in a class of at least 100 students each quarter.

Do it well. Sid was a handball player, and I play tennis. We were always kidding each other about who was better at the other's game, but never getting on the court to find out. Finally, one day we went to the handball court. The first game went about as expected—I was quicker then he, but he knew more about the game. During the contest, he kept complimenting me on my speed and my occasional good shot. He won that game, about 21−14. I then got lucky and real hot, and shut him out, 11−0 in the second game. Still, lots of compliments and lots of enjoyment. Naturally, during the next few days, I made an occasional snide comment about aging athletes and the like, which he merely laughed off. A week later, we went out for another quick game. Still full of kind words, and delighting at my agility, he ran me off the court, about 21−6. Do it well. Enjoy it fully, but do it well. We never did get around to playing tennis.

It's difficult to summarize the teacher-student relationship with Sid. Always very much alive—the true energy source of an often draining psychology building. Encouraging, sensitive, and supportive. During my first quarter at Florida, I went through a very private period of discouragement and depression. He recognized this without any comment from me, and on a particularly gloomy Friday afternoon, I discovered a little note on my desk. He mentioned how much work I had been doing, and that it was going well. But more importantly, it was a confirming statement that I was an important person to him, coming at a time when I was hurting. It was the only note I received from Sid, but as usual, his timing was superb and it helped me turn some things around and truly reinvent my perspective.

Most of all, Sid as a teacher was his own fully human person. As he wrote of himself in the *Transparent Self*, "I don't have a special 'researcher self', a 'therapist self', a 'teacher self', and a 'personal self'. These are names for places to do my thing" (1971, p. 169). This, I guess, was Sid's major statement to me: that human growth was a constant process of beginning new projects while integrating the old, developing new ways of being, while weaving conflicting social roles into one, larger being. He was always active, always challenging, and that laughter—he always had that laughter in his eyes.

References

Jourard, S. M. *Healthy personality: An approach from the viewpoint of humanistic psychology.* New York: Macmillan, 1974.

Jourard, S. M. *The transparent self: Self-disclosure and well-being* (Rev. ed.). New York: Van Nostrand, 1971.

Sid Jourard—
The Compassionate
Colleague

TED LANDSMAN

*T*his book is in tribute to a man of our times who could not wait for time to change the channels of his profession but who took its future into his own hands and helped make a science of white rats into a science of tender, loving, angry, ecstatic, joyful, tearful, saddened, and frightened, in other words, human, entirely human beings.

Sidney Jourard was a joyous, irrepressible, mischievous, mystic of a man who was a powerful mover of hearts and of thoughts, of ideas and of truths. The body image first excited him, then the idea of a self that was open, that did not seek to hide itself from its friend, its lover, its partner, the transparent self. Then authenticity became his spoken and written vigorous ambition to therapist and to client. It became a watchword of the third force in psychology—a relentless guerilla type intellectual and sentimental movement that reached beyond behaviorism, that loved and left psychoanalysis, and that sang paeans to a new trinity, existentialism, phenomenology, and humanism, all of which were enriched by this surprisingly, severely self-disciplined but always forceful and forever free spirit.

And out of that crazy, delightful cacophony of theory and philosophy of science and mysticism, the voice of Sidney Jourard was heard, a voice of courage and of caution, a voice of excitement and of balance, declaiming, founding, structuring, not a movement but a science. He disciplined himself to complete research projects on touching, self-concept, self-disclosure, and high level functioning. Was his work finished? He died in a tragic accident. Long before he had begun conceptualizations he wanted to research of enspiriting, of transcendent behavior, of the healthy personality, and in his last week of life, he reinvented renewed purpose for his life with a project to develop a humanistic political party and another one to create a complex grid of studies centering about the various relationships of authenticity between experimenter and subject.

His intense personal and professional friends are a strange mishmash, many of whom are the contributors to this volume. In addition to these selected writers flowed an odd brotherhood of soothsayers, yogis, philosophers, psychologists, I among them. The hand of Sidney Jourard labored to fashion a coherent but still human science.

His heart was where human history had wept, and his mind was in its transformation to joy. His soul was with man's yearning for God and for the heights of *menschlichket*, of personhood He wrote, he spoke, he shared, he encouraged, he enspirited the papers and the shared searches for the full human meanings in thought and feeling and science. This new science, this old science redefined, these grand words, those grander hopes and dreams and visions—they also are some evidence that one time, even in our days, Sidney Jourard walked proudly and joyously on the face of this earth.

Index